*Compliments of:*

CHRIS HEINRICH
REGAL CAPITAL PLANNERS LTD.
203-2495 LANCASTER RD.
OTTAWA, ONT. KIB 4L5
(613) 737-7767

*Happy investing !*

# Why I
# Invest in
# Mutual
# Funds

# Acknowledgements

My thanks to The Investment Funds Institute of Canada, formed in 1962 as The Canadian Mutual Funds Association. Its membership now represents virtually all 700 investment (Mutual) funds that manage over $140 billion in assets of approximately 4,000,000 Canadian investors. I appreciate their continuing representation of the industry, as well as their informational and educational programs. However, they will have to forgive my calculated decision to use throughout this book the term "mutual funds" rather than "investment funds."

In any financial business, numbers are very simple units, that when used properly, can portray strong messages. I am indebted, as always, to Coby Kobayashi for his flawless compilation of the figures used in my work.

My special thanks to those who edited, re-wrote, and up-dated the mountain of material contained in my original weekly newspaper columns which appeared in newspapers over a six-year period.

FOURTH EDITION

# Paul Rockel

# Why I Invest in Mutual Funds

ISBN 0-9692603-0-X


5  6  7  8  9  10  BP-74  1  0  9  8


Printed and bound in Canada
HMS Features Inc.
201 Consumers Road #106
Willowdale, Ontario
M2J 4G8

Cover Design and Art Direction: Marc Melanson

FIFTH PRINTING 1995

This book is dedicated to my wife and children,
who in my life, are my most precious assets.

# Table of Contents

# Foreword

"Dear Mr. Rockel,

"I am writing to express my thanks and share with you the 'success story' we have had with our investments and Sophia Roemer. On April 30, 1970 we completed the sale of our family home and property in Cooksville for approximately $100,000. We had been allowed to stay in our home until we could find another suitable place, and the mortgage payments we received just barely covered the cost of maintaining our father in a nursing home when he became too difficult to look after at home.

"As a result we had about $50,000 with which to buy a new home (cash to mortgage), leaving us about $25,000 to invest.

"At this time we became acquainted with Sophia Roemer, who persuaded us to invest in Canadian Trusteed Income Fund. Our investment grew steadily and we paid off our mortgage on our present home in 1972. When the bond market started to drop, we took Sophia's advice again and transferred our funds into the Industrial Group and Templeton Growth Fund — we added Trimark later.

"To make a long story short, I calculated that our original investment of $25,000 in 1970 has now grown to about $126,750 based on Aug. 2 newspaper quotations. In addition to this, we have been withdrawing a total of $300 a month from two of the funds.

"Recently I decided I should discuss taking out an RRIF with Sophia. She came to the house, spent about three hours going over the matter thoroughly with us, and as a result, I have decided to wait until reaching 71 years of age, and have arranged to have my company pension cheque deposited into my RRSP.

"We are absolutely delighted with the consideration, service and informed advice we have received from Sophia. Without her help, our senior years would not be as worry-free as they are now.

"Sincerely, Christina Crowley."   (Aug. 21, 1984)

# Introduction

Over thirty years ago I set a goal for myself. It was to try and help as many Canadians as possible achieve a fair measure of wealth, to encourage them to own a piece of Canada, and, therefore, to have a measure of control over their own destiny. If we buy back our industries, we will not only keep the ownership here, we will keep the profits in Canada. These profits would be spent, hopefully within Canada, subsequently making our country and ourselves more wealthy.

But you say, "I don't know anything about investing in Canada. I've never bought a stock in my life. I haven't the slightest idea of what to do."

When I started out, neither did I. But today I have ownership in most of Canada's major banks, its major industries, and even in some profitable businesses throughout the world. All the profit comes back to me to spend here. It helps create employment.

No, I don't know the first thing about the industries I have shares in. In fact, I don't even know the names of over 90% of them, and frankly, I don't even care. I revel in driving with my wife through a prosperous town and seeing a thriving business;

I wonder out loud, "Do we own a piece of that industry?" You see, I've done my investing through mutual funds.

I have also shared my investment philosophy with thousands of readers of Canadian weekly newspapers. The hundreds of my financial columns seen across the country have brought thousands of letters to my desk. Most of these writers want more information on mutual funds. And more than one has suggested a book on the subject.

It is my hope, that the compilation of these columns into book form, will benefit the reader, by showing how a measure of wealth can come your way. Thus taking me closer to my goal of putting more and more Canadians financially in control of their own destiny.

*Paul Rockel*

# 1

# Earning
and
Saving

# Only two ways to earn income

There are only two ways that any living person can earn an income. One is *person at work* and the other is *money at work*. The problem is that most of us never get around to developing that second income. We start our earning career with only the *person at work*. And if we live long enough to retire, we will have only the second income to rely on, namely, *money at work*. It's these in-between years that decide if we will retire in dignity and comfort or to a bare existence. During these in-between years we should make sure we have *both* methods of earning income under our belts.

Unless you inherit money or win a lottery, the only way you can have money at work is by saving a part of what you earn by working. We know of no other way. In retirement this saved money at work will become a valuable source of income.

Here are the only sources of income available to you after retirement.

1. Money you and/or your employer forced you to save into the company pension plan.

2. Money the Government forced you and your employer to save into the Canada Pension Plan.
3. Money the Government extracted from you in taxes and now will pay back in the form of the Old Age Pension.
4. The income from your personal savings.

Experience has shown that Government benefits such as (2) and (3) have never given anyone in retirement, more than a meagre subsistence. Some company plans leave a great deal to be desired. And some people (particularly those who have changed employers often) have very little or no company pension benefits.

Therefore, if we wish to continue the standard of living we've become accustomed to, it is entirely up to each of us, as individuals, to provide our own *money at work* for our retirement. You don't have to earn a large salary to have *money at work*. A young person of 21 saving $50 a month at an annual average return of 15% would, at age 65 be worth over $2 million. The one who waits until 50 to start saving $50 a month (at the same rate) would be worth only $30,000 at age 65. The younger you start saving, and earning that second income, the better. The 21 year old can retire on 10% of his savings. Without touching the principal amount he would have $200,000 to spend every year. Similarly the 50 year old would (at the same rate) have to live on $3,000 annually.

# Two ways to spend

Every dollar you earn can be spent in only two ways.

You can spend it on things that are consumed and lose their value or you can spend it on things that increase in value. Most of our dollars are spent on goods that depreciate in value or get 'used up'. We buy cars, appliances, and fur coats, that are worthless after a few years. We go out for dinner and entertainment; we take vacations; and immediately we're back home and the enjoyment fades, we are left with only the memory.

These things that give us immediate benefit are important to our lives. But we need not spend all of our worked-for income on expendables. If you want to have investment income for your non-working years you must decide to put a portion of your regular income aside for investment. If you never invest to create wealth, you never will have wealth.

# Pay yourself first!

It's not what you earn that counts, but what you keep for yourself. In my many years in the investment industry I have run across many people who gave the appearances of wealth, and in reality they had next to nothing. They were earning big incomes, but they were spending their money as fast as they could earn it. They were making regular payments on things like cars, stereos, TV's, and vacations. Although they 'owned' these things, they were actually decreasing in value as they were paying for them. But we've run across others who earned just a nominal income, saved part of that income, and were on their way to true wealth.

Guess who were the happiest?

You're right. The savers. They could see their financial lot improving. In most cases members of the family were much happier. The spenders were often dissatisfied, always wanting more things, but never seeing themselves as out of debt. The things they loved to have would lose value and have to be replaced.

Do you pay yourself first?

There is an easy, almost painless way to do it. These people will save through a PAC. That stands for Pre-Authorized Cheque. Many of us use PAC's to make the monthly payments on our homes. The bank or trust company, once authorized, sends the prescribed amount to the mortgage holder every month. We should do the same with our 'pay yourself first' savings. Then you should INVEST those regular payments.

# Living on less

The secret to becoming wealthy is not necessarily to earn a big income, but to start saving a part of what you earn, as soon as you start earning. You say, however, "I can't. I need everything I earn just to live on." So you go on earning and spending everything. And eventually have nothing to show for all that earning except some obsolete and devalued 'essentials'. What if you were not paid all you earned each week, and were forced to live on less? Could you do it?

Do you know that every dollar you spend is invested in something that either goes up in value or down in value. Unfortunately most Canadians spend the majority of their dollars on assets with only the appearance of wealth — like fine clothes, fancy cars, audio and video systems. These items may make us feel rich, but in reality these items depreciate each and every day.

Before purchasing anything we should ask ourselves "What will this item be worth ten years from now? Will this item enhance our goal of retiring on schedule? Or will it detract? Is this item something we absolutely *need*? Or is it something that we merely *want*?

Have you ever thought of yourself as a poverty seeker? In this day of saturized advertising, we are urged constantly on our TV's, radios, in our newspapers and magazines, to want more and more, and to spend more and more. But if we spend everything we earn on only the things we want, we are in fact poverty seekers.

On the other hand the wealth seekers know that they don't need instant gratification. They can do without a certain item knowing that by investing the same amount of money now, they will eventually be able to buy whatever they want, without harming their financial security. The wealth seeker can sacrifice; the poverty seeker is self-indulgent.

# Force yourself!

Saving isn't easy for young couples. Almost every husband and wife just starting out could justify the claim that they need every cent coming in for actual living expenses. The trouble is, that after ten years of marriage, they could still make that claim. A couple's living standard has a way of keeping up with the size of the pay cheque. If there are two pay cheques, the expenses usually go up accordingly. There's only one way for young people to have some financial security in their marriage and that's to put a small percentage of the family income aside *before* they start to spend.

I, too, once spent all my money on things for myself, my wife, and young family, but thirty-five years ago, I convinced myself that part of what I earn is mine to keep. I started saving and investing a little bit of every dollar I made. I became a wealth seeker, and continued investing until my financial goals were met.

Several years ago I visited Japan, and was astounded to learn that most employees were paid only three-quarters of what they earned. The balance was paid to them once or twice a year. So, although it was earned, it seemed like a bonus when they saw it. If they actually earned $1000 a month, they would be paid $750 with the other $250 being held back for payment later in the year. In effect employees were being forced to save and to live virtually on $750 a month. They all seemed able to do it. What happened then when they received their 'bonus' cheques? Most of them took the money and invested it. In many cases they bought shares in their own company or other Japanese companies.

Thanks to this hold-back system of paying salaries, Japan has the highest saving rate per person of any nation in the world. It is reported that they save approximately 21% of what they earn. And despite the fact that over past years Japanese workers received considerably less than we on the North American continent, they are much wealthier, on an average, than most of us. All because they were forced to save and then invested those savings.

In travelling to various cities, and visiting the exotic resorts throughout the world, I am constantly amazed at the number of Japanese tourists. They are well-dressed, stay in the finest hotels, and of course, carry the best cameras. They can afford it, because they saved and invested part of what they earned...regularly.

If you force yourself to save and invest, some day you will travel the world. It does take money. But those travellers are not necessarily huge wage earners. They started early to save something regularly.

# Are Canadians different?

I heard a saying the other day that got me thinking. "Give an American a dollar and he'll say, 'Where can I invest it for the best return?'; give a Canadian a dollar and he'll ask, 'Where can I invest it safely?'"

Are we that different? When it comes to financial planning, I guess we are. We seek the safety aspect; our cousins to the south think about the potential profit. Maybe that's why they control so much of our industries. They take the chances, while we seek the safe route.

# Earning interest

If we analyze our saving habits, we must admit that depositing our savings in a financial institution such as a bank, trust company or credit union, is allowing them to do with those dollars as they please...as long as they pay us interest. We are actually 'renting' them our money. The same is true when we 'lend out' our money on a mortgage.

Because that's all we were ever taught, most Canadians are doing nothing all their lives, but 'rent' their savings. I don't rent out my money because I can't afford to earn interest.

If you think about it, you'll see that none of us can afford to earn interest. It's because of the erosion that takes place through the 'twin evils' of inflation and taxation. Today, if I receive 8.5% interest or 'rent' and I'm in the 50% tax bracket, all I have left after taxes is 4.25% on my money. And if inflation rises above 4.25%, I have no gain in purchasing power whatsoever. That's why I don't rent out my money to earn interest.

## Two ways to invest

Now, there are only two ways of putting money to work for you.

The one most commonly used, as we've discussed is to loan or 'rent' your savings out to a financial institution that pays you interest on your loan. The problem is that all 'rented' money earning interest is subject to income tax. The after-tax and inflation-adjusted figure is your real rate of return.

The other way of investing is to 'own' something. That is, use your savings to buy something that is considered an investment. This means buying a business, shares in a company, or income property like an apartment building.

Do you get interest from owning an apartment building? No. When you 'own' something you earn a profit (income from the rent, minus the expenses of upkeep, utilities and taxes). Another word for profit is dividend. You know that term from your friends who own shares in the stock market.

When you decide you don't want to own those shares or the apartment house and they are sold at a profit (selling price minus the purchase price), you have made a capital gain. Fortunately, the government favours our investing as an owner and gives a relatively low rate of tax on dividends, and capital gains are subject, normally to three quarters of our individual tax rate (vs. 100% of interest being taxable).

If you are like me, and want the lower taxed return of dividends and capital gains, you must 'own' something that, in our economic system, normally appreciates in value. Some of my money pooled with thousands of others' savings in mutual funds is being invested in large blocks of Canadian industries every single day. And it's being watched over by investment experts. When I want a portion of my money I can get it any time I want. And when I get it I will have a virtually tax-free gain.

I like owning rather than loaning.

They tell me that, collectively, we Canadians have enough money to buy back, and own virtually all industry in Canada. But we're afraid to invest because those ownership investments are not guaranteed. So what do we do? We let our savings sit in financial institutions like banks and trust companies.

I think it's an awful price we pay for those fears. The price of all those profits leaving the country to be spent elsewhere. Because a lot of the owners of Canadian industries are not Canadian. Are you willing to buy back Canada? I am.

# Time and money

What's the formula for financial success?

It's quite simple. *Time + money × rate of return.* Do you know which of these is the most important? I'll tell you this story, then see if you have an answer.

Person 1 decided at age 25 to save $50 a month. S/he used mutual funds that, let's say grew at 15% a year for 40 years. At the age of 65 s/he had put away $24,000 but the value was $1,227,571. Yes that's ONE MILLION, TWO HUNDRED AND TWENTY-SEVEN THOUSAND, FIVE HUNDRED AND SEVENTY-ONE DOLLARS.

Person 2 was 45 years old and decided to catch up to Person 1. So s/he saved $100 a month for 20 years until age 65. The total investment was also $24,000. If the investment earned the same 15% annually the value at age 65 would be $141,372.

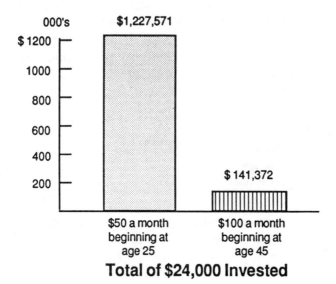

Person 1 had accumulated $1,086,199 MORE than Person. 2. They both invested the same amount of money at the same rate of return. So, I'll ask again. Which is more important? The amount of money, the rate of interest, or the amount of time?

All three ingredients are important, but the most important one appears to be TIME. The earlier you start saving, the more you will have at the end. After all Person 1's first $50 worked 39 years and 11 months. Person 2's first $100 worked only 19 years and 11 months.

How is it that we continually run across people who say, "I can't save a part of what I earn. After all I need that car, the money to date, and have a good time." Later they say, "I need all I'm earning to buy furniture and things for the apartment for me and my mate." Or "I can't save because there are children to support, the mortgage to pay off, and then university for the children." It goes on and on.

# You can't catch up to TIME.

Every day that passes is gone...and can never be reclaimed. If you haven't saved a little bit today, maybe 5% or hopefully 10%, you will not have the opportunity again. You cannot buy yesterday back!

Person 2, while saving double the dollar amount each month, lost both 20 years of TIME *and* over ONE MILLION DOLLARS.

# Interest rates

Compounding. It's a strange word with an awful lot of punch. But most people if they see a statement that says 15% compounded really have little comprehension of what it means.

Let's examine 'compounded' with the traditional investor "A" and investor "B". "A" is the one who earns investment income and spends it. "B" is the one who leaves it to compound. We'll use a 15% rate of return for each of them. Let's assume both "A" and "B" are 45 years old, and they each have $10,000. Let's look at the mathematics.

"A" earned $1,500 each year ($10,000 × 15%) and spent that $1,500 each year. Over the course of the 20 years to age 65, he would have earned $30,000 ($1,500 × 20 years) and would still have his original $10,000. Add the two together and you get $40,000. Not too bad for an original investment of $10,000.

"B" also earned 15% annually on his $10,000. But he decided not to spend his earnings but to leave them each year to compound. As a result, the first year's earnings were added to his original $10,000 giving him a total value of $11,500. The next year he earned another 15% on that total, giving him a gain of $1,725. Add that to the previous $11,500 and he now has $13,225 on which to earn his 15% for the next year. And so it goes...year after year.

At age 65 investor "B" ends up with a value of $163,665. Yes, that's ONE HUNDRED AND SIXTY-THREE THOUSAND, SIX HUNDRED AND SIXTY-FIVE DOLLARS. That's a lot of words...and a lot of money from only $10,000.

In fact it's a gain of $123,665 more than investor "A" who didn't let his earnings compound and grow. "A" made a $30,000 total profit but spent it each year. "B" left his profits and gained $153,665. If "B" now went out and spent the same $30,000 that "A" spent, he'd still have $133,665 left.

They both earned the same rate of return, but only one used compounding. That's the power of compounding your earnings.

# Compound or simple interest

It always scares me as to how statistics can be used to create what I'll call improper impressions or, for that matter, 'false' impressions. How do they do that in the field of investments? They sometimes quote you SIMPLE INTEREST as the rate of return.

For example, a bank advertised that you would receive a 12% average gain on their RRSP in the next five years. The 12% was shown in large figures and in bold type. But if you read very closely the fine print following, it said "which is equivalent to 9.75% compounded annually."

We know of an unwary investor who chose that particular RRSP, where it locked-up his assets for 5 years. He expected 12% per year on his money. If he put in $1,000 he expected at the end of one year $1120.

But it turned out it wasn't that figure. It was worth only 9.75% more namely $1,075. True, the next year he earned another 9.75% on the larger sum, but it would never grow at more than 9.75%...not 12%.

In five years it would be worth $1,592. So you could say he gained $592 over his original $1,000. If you divide $592 by 5 (years) you come out with a SIMPLE ANNUAL AVERAGE of 11.8% which is close to the 12% that was advertised. But a simple average is not a true picture. It's a case where statistics can be used to give a false impression. That $1,000 wasn't earning 12%! It was only earning 9.75%!

When banks, insurance companies or even the government (as they have done in the past with C.S.B.'s) use the simple annual average rate of return over a given number of years, they are trying to make the interest rate appear better than it really is.

The mutual fund industry always uses the compounded average rate...always the lower of the two. They pride themselves on being completely honest and correct in all their advertising. They truly operate in a goldfish bowl where anyone can follow the prices quoted in the daily newspapers and they calculate their performance in true percentages.

# Can you afford to earn interest?

Even at 12%, I can't afford to earn interest.

In fact, when my son asked me to assume the mortgage on his newly-purchased home, my immediate answer was "No way! But I'll back you at the bank or trust company, if you wish." You see I can't afford to lose purchasing power each year.

As we have seen, the first thing to look at in contemplating investments, is the rate of return. But that's often the only thing that people consider.

The second thing to look at, is THE RATE OF RETURN *AFTER TAXES*. That is a very, very important point.

The third thing to look out for is the RATE OF INFLATION. These last two points, in the last several years, have made it a 'losing' proposition for me to earn interest. Let's look at why.

If you were to earn 12% per year in interest and have a taxable income of $30,000, you would be paying approximately 42% in taxes.

Therefore your 12% return would be reduced by (12% x 42% tax) 5%, leaving an after-tax return of 7%. If you are in the top bracket you are paying tax in excess of 52%, therefore your after tax return would be less than 6%.

Now let's look at inflation. Over the past 30 years it has averaged slightly less than 6% per year. True, there were many years in that period where inflation was only 2%, etc. but there were also years at 12%. If we deduct the inflation rate from the 7% after-tax return, we end up with a purchasing power gain of only 1%. For the person in the top tax bracket, deducting 6% inflation from 6% after-tax gain, leaves the investor with 0% gain.

Now let's suppose that the 12% return was in capital gains and dividends. With the lower income bracket ($29,590 or less) the after-tax return on dividends would be over 11%, vs. 8.7% on interest earnings. On Capital Gains the after-tax return would be 10% vs. 8.7% on interest earnings. For the top tax bracket, on a 12% capital gains the after-tax return would be 7.28% vs. 5.71% on interest earnings.

So you see, I would much rather have a 12% gain composed of dividends and capital gains (you get **both** with "ownership" investments), than earning 12% in interest. Because of the tax rules, I would have much more to spend after taxes than I would with the interest return.

Probably no-one has taught you the difference in taxing various kinds of returns. It's quite understandable, because the financial institutions we deal with day in, day out, such as banks, trust companies, and credit unions offer only one kind of return...and that is interest.

Well where, you ask, can I find capital gains and dividend investments. We'll deal with that in another chapter, but as you may already have guessed I prefer mutual funds.

# Capital gains

On "equity" holdings, such as share owner-ship of businesses, commercial real estate, etc. there are two types of potential for gain (or loss). One is capital gains (increase in value of the asset), only $^3/_4$ (75%) of which is subject to tax at your tax rate. The other is called dividends (profit) which has even more tax advantages than capital gains. An example, someone in the median tax range of 42% would pay that rate on interest earnings and wages, whereas on dividend earnings the tax would only be 25.5%.

If you receive a 10% return, of which half is capital gains and half is dividends, and were in the median tax bracket of 42%, you would have 3.725% after-tax return on the 5% dividend, and 3.43% on the 5% capital gain. The two added together mean your after tax return would be 7.155%, whereas earning 10% in interest the after-tax return would be 5.8%. Putting it in dollar terms, an investment return of $1,000 made up of $500 capital gains and $500 dividends would leave $715.50 after-tax spendable dollars, whereas an interest return of $1,000 would leave only $580 after-tax dollars to spend. It's the after tax rate of return that counts.

# Dividend income

What is a dividend anyway? It is the after-tax profit of a corporation paid to its owners or shareholders. After the taxes have been paid, both federally and provincially, the money that is left can be paid to the shareholders.

Let's assume there are only two shareholders of our company, you and me. The company must pay tax on it's profits, and what is left after paying those taxes, is distributed to we shareholders as a dividend to pay tax on again. That's double taxation. The conscientious government, realizing it isn't quite fair, has a complicated scheme called the Dividend Tax Credit.

What it does is give dividends to those with lower taxable incomes an almost tax-free income, especially in relation to interest-earnings. Here are the rates for an Ontario resident in 1993.

### After-Tax Return for Ontario Resident – 1993
(Assumed Investment Return of $1,000)

| Taxable Income | Dividends | Interest |
| --- | --- | --- |
| $6,750 to $29,590 | $926 | $726 |
| $29,591 to $52,193 | $745 | $581 |
| $52,194 to $59,180 | $729 | $556 |
| $59,181 to $63,315 | $665 | $504 |
| $63,316 to $67,776 | $656 | $490 |
| $67,777 and over | $646 | $476 |

# Times sure have changed

When I was a child, I was taught by my parents that the only safe investment I should ever make was to deposit my money in a savings account at a sound financial institution. There was supposedly no risk...and there was an assured gain.

What has changed? The aspect of loaning out our money is still the same. If we deposit $100 into an account and make 3% on it, we, like my parents did, would earn $3 in a year. What has changed is taxation and inflation. My parents got to keep that $3 because they were not taxed on it. And there was no inflation to erode away the value of that $100. Today, with inflation having averaged 5.89% over the past 30 years, I would be losing almost 3% per year in purchasing power **plus** loss due to taxes. Interest rates are falling from their high of a few years ago, but maybe I can make 8% on my deposits. That's all right as long as I don't have to pay any income tax. However, if my salary puts me into a 50% tax bracket, I'm now down to 4% after-tax dollars earned on my deposit. With inflation taking the purchasing power away from my interest earned dollars I have made no actual gain on my $100. My parents got to keep and spend their $3. But with inflation and taxation today, even an 8% interest rate gives me *no* spendable improvement on my investment, but rather an "after-tax and inflation" loss of purchasing power.

Sorry, mom and dad, your advice no longer fits. Times have changed. We can't afford to 'loan'... we must 'own.'

# 2

# Safe
# Investments

# What investments are safe?

The investments that we consider 'safe', such as term deposits or GIC's in banks and trust companies, treasury bills, residential mortgages, and long-term bonds, have all proven to return considerably less than the Toronto Stock Exchange average of 300 stocks.

True, the term deposits never lost any money...and at one point were paying over 18% a year. The same goes for the mortgages; they always gave a positive return, again sometimes over 18%.

But those 18% rates were short term and were available for only a few months. It's true that some people locked up their money for 5 years. But others who could not find additional dollars or their previous term deposits did not come due at that time, were unable to take advantage of that fabulous rate of return.

Mr. John M. Templeton, recognized around the world as one of the wisest money managers, believes that all people have a common objective — to produce the maximum total return, after taxes and after inflation. He says that when people say they want safety, they *mean* safety in terms of purchasing power. If they want true safety in terms of dollars, he suggests they invest in guaranteed certificates or a money market mutual fund.

Mr. Templeton adds: "It's true that some people say, 'I want safety,' but 90% of them don't mean that. What they really mean is that they want to have some purchasing power even after inflation and taxes. Our belief is that in the next 35 years the cost of living is going to be 16 times as high as it is today. Therefore, if you invested in guaranteed certificates or a money market mutual fund, you would really suffer. But, if you invested in a common stock mutual fund it should at least keep pace with that increase in the cost of living.

"You should not say that a retired person needs a fund that pays a high dividend. What you want for *any* person is the mutual fund that's going to produce the maximum total return — income plus capital gains. As a person gets older he may need more income to live on, but he would be wise to invest for capital growth rather than high dividends. The most promising stocks usually pay out little or nothing in the form of income. So the person who needs safety should invest in a well-managed common stock mutual fund."

I agree full-heartedly with Mr. Templeton. Let's compare some 10-year rates of return.

| Investment | Compounded Average Return | $10,000 After 10 years |
|---|---|---|
| Canada Savings Bonds | 9.20% | $24,112 |
| Term Deposits | 8.60% | $22,820 |
| Treasury Bills | 9.63% | $25,078 |
| S+P 500 Index | 15.01% | $40,490 |
| TSE 300 Index | 9.74% | $25,330 |
| Templeton Growth (1984-1993) | 14.75% | $39,585 |

The rate of return of the first four investments may have varied within the ten-year period but within the specific term the rate would be fixed. For example, one term deposit could have been yielding 10.61% for five years and another 11.16% for five years. Likewise the Stock Exchange figure would reflect periodic fluctuation as well as static intervals. The specific mutual fund quoted actually had a high return of 35.1% (in 1985) and low of −13.6% (in 1990). So the compounded gain is averaged over the ten-year period.

# Guaranteed investments

We're all brought up to save. And sometimes to open a savings account. Today our bank deposits are guaranteed by the government up to $60,000 per account. And most of us don't worry about that because we don't have that much entrusted to the banks, anyway. Some prefer to spend it and others prefer to invest it. Myself, when I have the money, I would not let it sit in an interest bearing account. I do keep small amounts for paying regular bills and for vacations. But I can't afford to earn interest, guaranteed or not. Which of the above investments would you say are guaranteed? Certainly not the Standard and Poor 500 Stock Index (S+P 500). Yet over the last ten years on the S+P 500 I could have made (on a $10,000 investment) $17,670 more ($40,490 versus $11,810) than the term deposits would have yielded within the same period. One is not only 'safe'...it's guaranteed. So are the treasury bills. But which return would you rather have?

# Afraid to invest

We Canadians seem to be able to think long-term (15, 20, 25 years) when we pay for our homes. We get married to hopefully live 'happily ever after'. And we expect to have our children with us for 15 to 25 years before they move out on their own.

But when it comes to investments, if they don't make money almost immediately, we tend to avoid them. Maybe that's why most of us don't invest in Businesses (stocks). If you're like me, you don't know anything about investing in stocks and bonds, and are afraid to try. Also, we have noted that they go up *and* down. When they go down we figure we lose our money. We get scared and are afraid to look at the long term. In spite of the 'downs' or losses, the average is much better over the long haul.

I know nothing of the market, so I use equity mutual funds for my investing. Many funds have done even better than the TSE 300 Index average. And I feel confident that the full-time people, who know what to do and when to do it, are looking after my dollars better than I could on a part-time basis.

I also like getting (over ten years on a $10,000 investment) that extra $15,000 or so, over and above the other methods of investing (compared on page 51).

Wouldn't you?

# Real estate

Most Canadians, if they can possibly afford it, purchase a home to raise their families, to plant their gardens, and to live their daily lives. But is the purchase of real estate as an investment, the best thing to do?

We know that many people believe that real estate is the best investment one can make. In particular many new Canadians feel strongly about this and plow all of their savings into real estate.

Mr. 'Coby' Kobayashi, a former real estate agent, now a friend of mine in the mutual fund industry, compiled some statistics that we find very interesting. You'll find a complete chart in the appendix, (page 166) but let me point out the value comparison between a Toronto house in 1967 and 1993 and, over the same period, a GIC, a growth mutual fund, and the inflation value.

|  | Dec 67 | Dec 93 | Annual Compound Rate of Return |
|---|---|---|---|
| Inflation | $24,078 | $117,554 | 6.35% |
| Toronto House | $24,078 | $206,490 | 8.62% |
| GIC's | $24,078 | $267,151 | 9.70% |
| Mutual Fund | $24,078 | $1,744,412 | 17.9% |

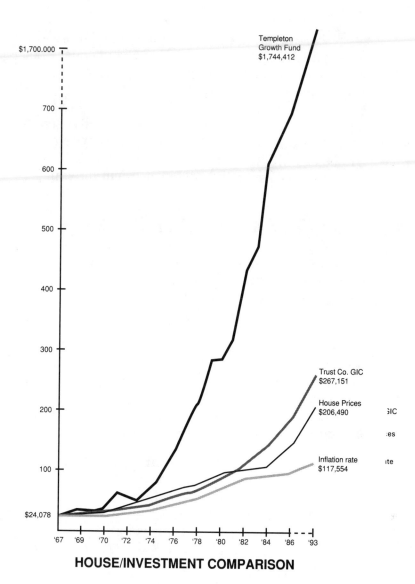

**HOUSE/INVESTMENT COMPARISON**

All the investments beat out inflation, which shows us that today we need $117,554 to equal what $24,078 would have bought 26 years ago. And the house value grew to $206,490, the GIC grew to $267,151, but the mutual fund grew to $1,744,412. The same dollar amount was invested in all cases over the same period, but the fund return was over $1,500,000 MORE than the house return

Is real estate the best investment for you?

# Do I pay off my mortgage?

A lot of advisors say "Pay down your mortgage and save a great deal on your house costs." They are right mathematically.

But I disagree with the philosophy. You see, it is not the people who 'pay off' quickly that get ahead, but the investors who save, and invest those savings, that end up wealthy. I say, don't pay off your house in a hurry, but rather extend that mortgage as long as you can. Pay it off with 10¢ dollars (thanks to inflation) 20 or 30 years from now.

I remember my dad, when he sold the house I was born in, saying to me: "You know, when I built this house in 1926, I borrowed almost $3,000 from your grandfather. Now, 20 years later, I'm selling it for $11,000. That means I'm now going to pay your grandfather off with less than 30¢ dollars. It doesn't make me feel good."

# Borrow, then pay the mortgage

Another example: Mr. A and Mr. B each have houses with 25 year mortgages and monthly payments of $500. After three years their income had increased sufficiently for them to save $60 a month. Mr. A decided to put his saving toward his mortgage. He was thus able to cut down his term remaining from 22 years to 15 years. He was pleased. Mr. B invested his savings in Templeton Growth Fund, and in the same 15 year period he saw his investment grow to $56,720. At this time he decided to go on a monthly withdrawal plan of $500 to make his mortgage payments. He paid nothing out of his wages.

Both Mr. A and Mr. B paid off their mortgages. But Mr. B still had his pool of capital growing. Chances are that because the fund earned over 15% per year during the withdrawal period, and he was withdrawing less than 11% a year, that his value was growing an average of 4% a year. In addition to his withdrawals, his investment grew to over $80,000 by the time the mortgage was paid off.

Mr. A had his house paid for. So did Mr. B. But in addition Mr. B had his $500 income and his investment kept growing. Mr. A, the payer had his house Mr. B, the investor has his house, the $500 monthly income, and probably $80,000.

Both had paid out exactly the same amount of money in the same time.

# Stay out of the stock market

Between 1955 and 1976, 'Smiling Bruce' Hanson was a stockbroker. He then formed an investment counselling firm and advised his clients. "Unless you have a lot of money, and want to make a career of it, stay out of the stock market. You can't win as a small investor. You don't have enough money to diversify. Even if your stocks do well, by the time you pay the brokers, you can lose. Investing is not a part-time do-it-yourself activity."

He went on to say he didn't know why anyone would invest on their own unless they were willing to give up everything else and make it a full-time job. Mr. Hanson's advice was to determine what your long-term objectives are, then plan for that. His recommendation for the small investor is to seek out an independent mutual fund specialist.

Brokers may hold themselves out to be advisers, but their job is to sell securities. The independent mutual fund salesperson, while also earning a fee on sales, will seek out only the best funds to maximize your savings dollar. If the salesperson doesn't perform, through the recommended funds, they will lose you as a client.

# A look at Canada Savings Bonds

The Canadian government raises money every year through selling Savings Bonds. They do help you save, but the money raised is used to pay the interest and principal on the bonds coming due and being cashed. If someone asked you for a loan to repay the principal and interest of a loan that was made to repay the principal and interest of a previous loan, would you provide money for such an unstable pyramid? Why then, do so many patriotic citizens not hesitate to purchase Canada Savings Bonds?

Every year the government asks 'Peter' to fulful the promise made to 'Paul' in previous years. If 'Peter' won't voluntarily purchase CSB's, the government will take the money from him through direct and indirect taxation. In the process the government cheats 'Paul' by paying him back with debased currency worth less in purchasing power than his original money.

These are the sentiments of a Mr. R. Martilla writing to the editor of The Financial Times of Canada. Because of this 'debasement' called inflation I can't afford to own CSB's. Can you?

Canada Savings Bonds are a safe investment, you say. They are guaranteed by the government. Do you know the only two ways that the government can find money to pay you back with interest? One is through further taxing of you and me, and the companies we work for, and two is printing money. If all the companies listed in a mutual fund portfolio were to go bankrupt and could not pay their taxes, and the employees who lose their jobs won't be paying taxes, then money might have to be printed to pay the principal and interest on those bonds. This would cause severe inflation. You could cash in your bonds, but would they be able to buy a loaf of bread?

# Buy shares in the bank

A few years ago W. Rankin Hodgins of Alberta wrote to Mr. A. White, a Vice-President of the Bank of Montreal.

"In 1952 my father retired from farming with his house and roughly $100,000. He invested in Canada Savings Bonds. Instead of this type of investment, had father bought $100,000 worth of Bank of Montreal shares, how many shares would we have today? If you can give me the dividend history over that period it would be appreciated. I personally have 1,600 common shares of Bank of Montreal and 500 of your preferred stock."

The answer from Mr. White in October 1983 stated: "In 1952 your father could have acquired roughly 3,400 shares, which after a five-for-one split in 1967, would be 17,000 shares today. The current market value would be $456,875. In computing this value, we have not taken into consideration a further $410,093 of dividends that would have been earned since that time." That $100,000 could have been worth $866,968 after the 31 years.

What about the $100,000 in bonds versus the bank's reply? Canada Savings Bonds were paying approximately 5% to 6% all the way through to the middle 60's. We know we have had some years above that, but on the average, if 8% had been achieved over the 31 years, it would mean $8,000 per year or $248,000 earned. Combine that with the original $100,000 and it makes $348,000. That's what the father ended up with, by 'loaning' his money to the Government. If he had invested in the Bank of Montreal shares, he would have been worth $866,968.

That's over half a million dollars more!

# Cashing in

A few years ago I read one morning in the Globe and Mail *Report on Business.*

Mr. Michael Wilson, Finance Minister, after hearing that Canadians have cashed in almost $5 billion worth of CSB's since November 1985 commented in the House of Commons, "I should say I think a large part of the redemption during this period has been related to the increase in interest rates." Last November $50.18 billion worth of bonds had been purchased. Figures released by the Bank of Canada on March 20, 1986 show $45.22 billion worth of bonds remained outstanding...a drop of $4.96 billion.

The Finance Minister seemed to be admitting that there were higher returns being paid on other investments. (Hopefully a few Canadians have been reading my articles.)

# How to buy GOLD

Gold. It has a magic sound. Gold conjures up visions of wealth and grandeur. We would all like to own some. It's been around as long as history, and has proven to be the only lasting investment.

I remember the meteoric rise in the price of gold from $200 an ounce to $800. What hurts now, is remembering those people lining up to buy at $750, then losing a good portion of the value when gold fell back to $300 an ounce. I'm willing to bet that 90 per cent of those people who bought at $750 and $800 didn't have any knowledge of the gold market. Neither do I. But I didn't buy. And I didn't lose.

I owned gold, just the same. Some of the mutual funds I own bought gold. I didn't worry whether it was a good time to buy or own gold. I didn't decide to buy and sell, but I made money on gold. The fund managers are the ones who bought at $200 an ounce, and then sold when it reached the

$700 and $800 range. I too got excited when it hit $800, but I don't trust my emotions.

That's why I use funds. They are managed by people who don't let their emotions make decisions. They look at hard facts, at history, at past patterns, and then make intelligent, not emotional, decisions.

Funds such as GoldFund, have as much as 60% in actual gold bullion. The other 40% may be invested partly in cash reserves or in ownership of some of the gold mining companies. Holders of GoldFund shares benefit in both ways. For those who want RRSP qualification, there is a sister fund called GoldTrust. There are many other gold-related funds that have been established in the past few years.

Gold certainly does have that magic aura about it. Owning it can make you tingle. But with the fund, I can invest as little as $1000, and get the same tingle as the big guys. I like it.

# 3

# Financial
# Planning

# What is financial planning?

It's taking the assets you already have...the money you now earn...the money you will earn in the future...and getting the best possible value out of them by reducing your taxes, and increasing your investment return...all without reducing your standard of living.

Who needs financial planning? Everyone; every last person who works; who is retired; or who has any investment income.

Before we go any further, let me give you an example which is based on factual past performance...figures that cannot be denied.

Nineteen years ago, three neighbours each decided they were going to save $100 a month. However, they each chose a different method of putting those savings to work. Neighbour 1 chose to save in a savings account at his bank earning 10%. Neighbour 2 chose to invest in a mutual fund called Cundill Value Fund. Neighbour 3 called in a financial planner who suggested that he go to his bank, borrow $10,000 at 12% interest (requiring payments of $100 a month). Then he advised that the $10,000 borrowed be invested into the same mutual fund...Cundill Value Fund.

At the end of the nineteen years, the three got together to compare notes. All three had paid out only $22,800 over the period. But they were astounded by the results.

No.1  saw the $22,800 grow to over         *$ 68,828*
No. 2 saw the $22,800 grow to over         $132,305
No. 3 saw the $22,800 grow to over $267,947
repay loan $ 10,000

$254,947 ... $254,947

(see pages 176 and 177)

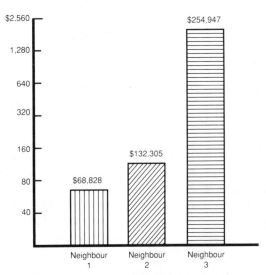

**Investment of $100 per month
for 19 years**

This man who had listened to his financial planner hadn't really saved $100 a month. Because he borrowed to invest, (he was in the 40% tax bracket) the Government gave him a tax deduction of $40 on each $100 paid in interest, making his "true cost" only $60 a month. And after repaying the $10,000 loan he was left with $254,947.

Which one would you rather be? Financial planning maybe is worthwhile.

(For complete details see tables on pages 176 and 177).

# Set goals

Have you got an idea as to what you want, the amount of dollars and possessions you would like to have, when you retire? Or are those 'ideas' only dreams?

Do you have any financial program or are you like the majority of people who simply drift along day by day. They get up, go to work, eat their meals, watch television, and go to bed. Then they repeat the same pattern the next day. And the next. Those who do live like that must lead a very dull and distressing life, not having any goals and purposes which they would like to achieve.

True there are personal goals that are not financial, such as giving your children and family love and affection. But we live in a world which also demands financial goals, because those children may want to go to university...and that costs money.

Why do you choose your clothes with such care? Women in particular scan the fashion pages to see what's latest in fashions and colours, then choose their clothing accordingly. Men choose their cars and possessions carefully too, going from place to place to get the best deal on the best model. Men and women drive all over looking at many, many homes before choosing their very own place to live.

But too few of us take much time to plan our financial security. Instead we take the easy way out and simply do not save for our future. Or if we do, we use the 'convenient' and 'guaranteed' method available at the institution where we deposit our regular employment earnings.

Why are we so careless about our future? And so fussy about our clothes, cars, and homes? We don't know.

# People don't plan to fail — they fail to plan

They tell us that only 2% of Canadians will end up with sufficient assets of their own to retire and maintain their previous standard of living. True, we don't need those assets of our own in Canada today because the government forces us to save by making us contribute to the Canada Pension Plan. It also taxes us extra so that we can receive the Old Age Pension when we retire.

But even with these benefits, they tell us only 5 out of every 100 people will be able to maintain their standard of living until they die. Yet, I believe, every Canadian can enjoy a measure of wealth, if they would only apply one simple rule.

*'Save a part of what you earn, and let the earnings compound.'*

When you retire, if you have followed that advice, you will have all the assets you need to retire in dignity.

# Financial failure

The renowned U.S. author and TV moderator Venita Van Caspel, says in her million-selling book 'The Power of Money Dynamics' that there are six reasons why so many people fail financially.

1. Procrastination. They will start tomorrow, next week, or next year, and thus never get to save.
2. Lack of a definite, established financial goal.
3. Ignorance of money's role in accomplishing goals
4. Not understanding and applying the tax laws.
5. Being sold the wrong kind of life insurance.
6. Failure to develop a winning attitude to money.

The wise ones among us are the ones who recognize and will try to correct our shortcomings. To me, financial failure is not being able to obtain the money I'll need to live on, when I stop working for a living. I intend to still be earning money, but I'll be earning it from my investments.

How much money do you need this year to live comfortably? And how many years are you from retirement? A lot of people, whose leisure years are way down the road, say they'd be happy with a million dollars. When I point out that, at 10% return, the million would produce an annual income of $100,000 they smile and are feeling quite content. When they tell me that they need $25,000 this year to live on, I get concerned. And so should they. Because at an average of just six percent inflation per year, and they are now 41 years old, that million dollars will not produce the equivalent income when they are 65. Today $25,000 is not a large sum of money, but in 24 years, it could take well over $100,000 to have the same spending power (and remember males, at age 65, are supposed to live another 17 years).

I don't want any of you to be a financial failure. Set an accurate financial goal for yourself and your family.

# Financial security

When you talk to a 25 year old they will usually tell you that they are going to 'make it'. They are going to retire at 50 and enjoy life. It's unfortunate, but more than 90% of Canadians who retire, even at age 65, do not have sufficient assets to have the standard of living they enjoyed while working. These people need government handouts like the Old Age Pension, Canada Pension, and hopefully a company pension plan. But will even these small amounts be able to match the ever increasing costs, the inflation factor? When you retire you should have an even better standard of living than you were used to while working. When you retire you will have the luxury of time...the time to travel and do the things you could never do before.

# Financial planners

Today we live in a world of specialists. We go to doctors, dentists, mechanics, lawyers, accountants, and on and on, because they are experts in their fields. You and I become experts at what we do in our daily occupations. As a result, we cannot be expert in all the others.

How could you and I possibly know all the tax implications that apply to us? It is generally known that most people pay more than they should in taxes each year...because they don't know all the rules and regulations.

But I know a person who will gladly review the past two or three years of an individual's tax return...for nothing. Yes, no charge, other than a percentage of the tax refund he finds. The person being reviewed would always have paid more taxes than necessary; so the reviewer would always get paid.

The smart person is the one who uses a financial planner to arrange his or her affairs *before* paying taxes. This is the preferred way to reduce your tax bite. And there are many methods of doing this.

It's important to reduce the effects of inflation on our lifestyle. A financial planner can help save us hundreds and thousands of dollars each year from this erosion. The financial planner can lay out a program to build wealth for you and me.

We all need a financial planner, whether we earn $20,000 or $200,000 a year. Forty years ago, the impact of taxation was minimal; the impact of inflation was minimal. Then we didn't need planners. Today financial planners are almost a 'must'.

# What does a financial planner do?

Let's look at what a financial planner might show you on the investment side. We'll use the example of Mr. A who invests on his own and Mr. B who listens to a financial planner. Each has the same assets.

In 1968 Mr. A had saved $10,000. He found an institution that gave him the 5-year GIC rate. According to the Bank of Canada Review average 5-year GIC rate, at the end of 26 years, the $10,000 would have grown to $110,948.

At the same time Mr. B listened to a financial planner and placed his $10,000 into Templeton Growth Fund. At the end of the same 26 years it was worth $710,462. That's about $600,000 more. (See table page 167).

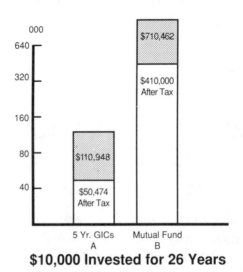

**$10,000 Invested for 26 Years**

Come income tax time. Mr. A had earned interest. His gain of $100,948 ($110,948 minus $10,000 invested) was subject to tax. If he were in the 50% tax bracket he would lose $50,474 in taxes. His net gain was $50,474.

Mr. B knew from his financial planner that his investment return would be made up primarily of Capital Gains and Dividends. Both of which are only partially taxable. If in the 50% bracket his tax payable would have been approximately $300,000. His after-tax value would be $410,000 or a net gain of $400,000 on his investment.

That's $350,000 more spendable gain than Mr. A. Mr. B was happy he consulted a financial planner. Wouldn't you be?

# The living estate

The 'living estate' is to ensure that if you live to a normal age, and hopefully into retirement, that you will have the assets to live those years in comfort...with the financial ability to enjoy life, travel and all the other amenities that come with freedom of time.

The 'death estate' is to ensure that if an untimely death were to occur, that you would have sufficient life insurance to provide for your family in the future.

These two 'estates' are the cornerstones of any financial plan. We think we know the 'best' way of incorporating these two 'estates' for virtually everyone.

First, we should plan ahead for 'living'. That means we should save a part of everything we earn. No matter what our circumstances, we should always live on less than we earn...and save the difference. The 21 year-old earning $1,000 per month who decided to save 5% per month would be putting aside $50. If this were done regularly until age 65 at 15% that person would have a 'living' estate of over $2,000,000. If he saved $100 a month, at 65 he would have an estate of over 4 million dollars.

The problem is, that most of us will not start saving at age 21. We're too busy buying cars, going out, and enjoying life now that we have started to work. Life is for spending, we say. If we wait to start saving until we are 30 the $50 a month would be worth, at 65, only $608,000. That's $1.4 million LESS than if we began saving only 9 years earlier.

Your 'death estate' should be in term insurance. But do you really need insurance if you have built a solid 'living estate'?

# Who needs life insurance?

All of us should have life insurance to protect our loved ones...and insurance companies are expert in deriving policy premiums that adequately reflect death rates. The premiums are designed so that there will be sufficient assets in the insurance company to pay out claims for those who are unfortunate enough to die at an early age and to cover those who live to a ripe old age. That's insurance.

In the past many policies were sold that included protection *and* savings. Trouble is, you couldn't collect on both. If you took out your savings, the policy was closed out and you had no more insurance. If your beneficiary collected, the amount paid was only the face value and you forfeited your savings. You did not get the insured face value *and* the savings. If you had borrowed from your policy, and died, your beneficiary would have received the face value of the policy *less* the balance of the loan. You simply could not collect on your SAVINGS and your PROTECTION. It was one or the other. Would you put money into a bank account, if the only way you could get your money back was "to pay interest" on your money, or cancel the account completely?

Today many insurance companies are now saying "Buy term...and invest the difference."

With term insurance you get just insurance. It is pure protection only. And it does not build up cash values. However, its cost is usually ¼ to ½ the amount of whole life (when the insured is younger and really needs the protection for a growing family). Because the premium is so much less, let's look at what happens when we invest the difference.

At age 25 a whole life policy of $100,000 would cost more than $1,100 a year; a term policy (adjustable) would cost $176 per year.

If the 'term' purchaser invested the difference in premiums for a period of 20 years at 15% he would have a savings value of $108,856. At this point he may no longer need insurance, considering that at death a beneficiary would fall heir to the $108,856.

When the owner of a whole life policy dies, he would leave his beneficiary the face value of $100,000. However, if they both lived beyond age 45, the 'whole life' owner would have to continue paying his $1,100 each year until death in order to keep his protection. At age 65 he would have paid $44,000 in premiums and still have only $100,000 of death protection.

The 'term' owner can then drop his insurance. He has paid out in 20 years $22,000 ($3,520 in premiums and $18,480 in investment) and currently has a value of $108,856. Without adding a single penny his worth will grow (at the 15% rate) in

20 years to $1,781,595. That's right. One million...Seven hundred and Eighty-one thousand Dollars.

At age 65, the 'whole' buyer paid $44,000; has a death *benefit* of $100,000. At the same time, the 'term' buyer paid $22,000; has an *estate* of $1,781,595.

So I repeat *buy term...invest the difference.*

Now I can hear the insurance people shouting "but the insurance payout is non-taxable." So isn't that great! You have $100,000 tax-free. Too bad you had to die for someone to spend it.

Even if the entire $1.7 million were taxed as a capital gain only 75% of capital gains are taxable. 75% of $1.7 million is $1,275,000 and if your tax bracket was 50% the tax would be $637,500. Deduct that from the $1.7 million and you have over $1 million left. You end up with NO insurance but can spend that amount while you're alive. And you have paid out a lot less than what the 'whole' owner did.

Which would you rather have? A death estate of $100,000...or a living estate of $1,000,000?

# Do we need any insurance?

Yes, I believe some insurance is a necessity. I still have life insurance. But it is decreasing yearly in its protection. I also save a part of what I earn.

I'm building a 'living estate' so that if I live to a normal age, I will have a sizable 'nest-egg' that will both keep me as long as I live and provide an estate for my wife and children if they live longer than I do.

Years ago a large insurance company ran advertisements featuring famous people...and how they planned to retire with various amounts of money. The ads were beautifully done. They were very factual and honest...giving details as to premiums, ages, cash values, and the amount of protection. The ad said I could retire at age 65 with $31,000.

So I took the figures in those ads and did my own calculations using simple mathematics. I discovered if I took the monthly premium of the advertised 'whole life' policy and I bought instead a decreasing 'term' insurance policy for the same face amount, then used the difference in premiums as a saving investment at 12%, I would end up, at 65, with NO insurance...but an amount of over $250,000. The total cost was actually lower than that for the 'whole life' plan.

I also discovered a weakness to my own plan. During the first ten years, my combined savings and decreasing insurance were not quite equal to the 'death' value of the whole life policy. But after the tenth year my combined value of savings and decreased coverage were in excess of the 'whole life' policy. What's more important, at age 65, when the insurance ran out, my value would be in excess of $250,000. I'd rather have no insurance and $250,000 than the advertised insurance benefit of $25,000 and a 'hoped-for' cash value of $31,000. Especially when I could collect on only one of the values...not both.

Actually, with my savings, I've earned even more than 12% because I put my savings into mutual funds.

# The ideal pension plan

Pensions! Many of us trust them to provide us with a worthwhile retirement. But do we know what our pension will provide us? Do we ever look at it? Do we even have a pension plan? Or will the government handouts be sufficient to accommodate us in dignity?

It's amazing how many of us just hope for these things, but never really look at what we are doing, or what our employer is doing.

A pension plan has four basic components
1. The contributions (yours and the employers)
2. The rate of return.
3. The overhead costs.
4. The ultimate benefits paid out.

The first three effect the fourth. In most pensions you have no choice as to any of those first three components. You take the plan as it was designed for the employer and accept it. Many employees have no idea as to the rate of return earned, the overhead costs, or even what the employer is contributing, if anything.

I believe there is a way to increase the rate of return, reduce costs, and give the employee flexibility in the size of the contribution. In fact I believe it to be the ideal pension package. More and more employers and employees, seriously looking at pensions, are agreeing.

That ideal pension plan is really not a pension plan but a group RRSP combined with a deferred profit-sharing plan for company contributions. It is actually an individual RRSP registered personally in your name, but paid for by a group cheque covering all employee contributions.

With this type of plan you can designate the amount you want contributed and deducted from your pay cheque. Usually it is a percentage of earnings, anywhere from 2% to 18%. No matter the amount it is your money and can be transported to a new job, if you change employers.

If you were to use mutual funds for these savings, according to past performance, you might average better than 15% per year. The employer can establish a DPSP (Deferred Profit Sharing Plan)...or percentage...or...contribute to your plan for its contribution toward your future retirement. This can either vary with profits from year to year, or it can be set at a fixed amount.

By utilizing these two methods, and investing in mutual funds the same amount you and your employer are now contributing to your pension, we can probably: 1). reduce considerably the overhead costs; 2). increase the rate of return on investment; 3), and increase the pension dollars available at retirement.

The employee who chooses to contribute through payroll deduction a total of $2,400 each year would find his after tax costs (depending on the tax bracket) would be between $1,200 and $1,800. But over 25 years at 15% he or she would have a value of $489,000. It could be transferred with you no matter how many times you changed employment during that time.

On top of that, add the company DPSP contributions. Suppose this portion was only $500 a year. After 25 years at 15%, it would be worth $122,000. The combined value would now be $611,000. Think of what it would be after 40 years of working. Does your present pension plan promise $60,000 a year during retirement. That's what a 25 year plan could earn you at 15% return.

# Get a 'trip map'

In a conversation with Brian Costello (many of you will have heard him on the radio or read his books), he suggested that the mutual fund industry and the financial planning industry are really "the travel agents of the financial world." He explained it like this:

"People wishing to take a vacation decide what they want to do, they pick a location, and then they make plans to get there. If going by air, they can phone an airline directly, and order their tickets. Or, they can go to a travel agent. Having described what they want to do, the travel agent can offer a choice of locations. Furthermore, rather than having one price on just one airline, the travel agent may have a dozen rates on different airlines. There could be a saving of several dollars, perhaps on a seat sale.

"In short, they will reach their destination, at possibly less cost, less frustration, and maybe at a better location than the one originally chosen. The cost of all these improvements is nothing. The travel agent gets compensated by the airlines and the resorts.

"Those who do financial planning for their clients, help choose a financial destination, show the ways to get there, by using investment rules and tax benefits that others probably don't know about."

In our business we help you set your goals of where you would like to be in the financial future. We often find people "drifting on the sea of life" without planning for their future. They say the government will look after them, or the pension at work is all they need. Then when they are facing the 'trip's end' and their retirement, they come to us and ask for help. It would be much easier to help them if they had sought a 'trip map' much earlier in their financial adventure of life.

# Know where you are going

Do you know how much money you will want or need ten years from now? Or at retirement age? Or would you like an early retirement, and sufficient money to do the travelling or the hobbies you've always wanted?

Have you given these things any thought? Or are you like so many thousands of Canadians who have no specific goals in life. They only wish to be taken care of.

In a book by Robert Allen, called Creating Wealth (published by Simon and Schuster), I read: "Set realistic goals and write them down!

"The 1954 Yale University seniors were asked, at the time of graduation, if they had set specific WRITTEN FINANCIAL GOALS. Only three percent had done so. About ten percent had specific goals, but they hadn't committed them to paper. The rest had no specific goals.

"Twenty years later they were re-surveyed. And you guessed it, the three percent outperformed the other 97% combined."

Those were top university graduates, and only three percent had written down their goals. Start planning for your future, particularly your financial future, because so much of what we wish to do, depends upon our financial ability. It does take a real plan, which lays out the mechanics required to meet your goals. I've heard many people say, "I'd like to be a millionaire" but it is only a 'wish' not a goal. A goal is a real desire for something particular, and if you let your mind dwell on that goal, by writing it down, and reading it every day, you soon come up with ways to achieve that goal.

It is wise to seek the help of professionals in laying out your financial goals. Those in the mutual fund industry, who are independent, can give you help and advice. It comes to you free. That's right, at no cost, to sit down with a consultant who can not only help set your financial goals but help you achieve them.

# 4

# Mutual
# Funds

# What exactly are they?

Mutual funds are professionally-managed investment enterprises in which people can pool their money and share in the growth and gain of a portfolio of stocks and securities. Because of the diversification within the portfolio, participants in the fund will own a small portion of a wide variety of investments.

# Who manages the funds?

Buying shares in a mutual fund is like hiring your very own investment counsellor. Each fund employs a full-time manager who constantly oversees the performance of each investment within the portfolio. There's no need to worry what or when to buy or sell. It's all done by someone who's trained and well-qualified to do the thinking and transactions for you.

# Are they liquid?

You can buy or sell shares in mutual funds any business day of the year. The Net Asset Value of most funds is calculated every day at the close of the markets. This value is used for purchase or redemption transactions the following day. There is no delay; your order is processed the same day.

# Who keeps the records?

All transactions, changes or transfers in holdings, capital gains, dividends, and tax-deferral plans are reported either monthly or quarterly. Annual detailed statements simplify the preparation of tax returns. Automatic regular deposits or withdrawals are options enjoyed by many.

# How have they performed?

For a better than average return, mutual funds are an excellent long-term investment vehicle.

Their short-term and long-term performance over various time spans are reported monthly in The Financial Times, The Financial Post and the Globe and Mail. No other investment provides this record of performance over the years. You can also track fund unit values (before and after purchase) in the large daily newspapers.

# How do I choose a fund?

There are over seven hundred funds in Canada. Some invest within Canada; others concentrate on the international market. Before you can make a choice, however, you should set your own financial goals, based on your particular age and objectives. There are aggressive funds for faster (although more volatile) gain; fixed income funds for the non-risk taker; and a wide choice between the extremes. There are growth funds, bond funds, income funds, equity funds, real estate and property funds, resource funds, balanced funds, and specialty funds. An independent mutual fund dealer can help draw up a financial plan to suit your needs, then recommend various combinations to meet those needs.

# Four reasons

Here are the four main reasons I have always recommended mutual funds to Canadian investors. First, mutual funds are designed for everyone, not just for the 'sophisticated' investor. The idea of pooling your bit of savings, and my bit, along with thousands of others, even large institutions and corporate investors, then having professional money managers look after the small bits and the big chunks all in that one 'pool' in the same manner, certainly makes sense.

Second, virtually everyone agrees that a person who spends full-time looking after investments, surrounding themselves with other money specialists, consults with them, before making decisions regarding 'our' pool of money, will probably do a better job than those of us who spend either an hour a day 'studying' the market or no time at all.

Third, mutual funds are always bought and sold at a 'calculated' or 'fixed' price. It's not a "I hope I can get so much" or "I hope I can buy it at such and such a price" as it is with stocks and bonds. By law, a mutual fund must value its holdings at the end of each day, divide that total value by the number of outstanding shares, and arrive at the 'fixed' price that is published in the newspapers.

When you and I purchase or sell shares in mutual funds, the transaction is always calculated at the 'next' price. In other words, if we were to purchase today, we would get the price that will be calculated at the close of the markets today (which is the same price that will appear in the papers tomorrow). The same goes for selling portions of any fund. The beauty of it is, we can figure out what our value is every day, if we wish. Just take the number of units or shares we own, multiply by the price quoted in the paper, and presto we know our value.

Fourth, with mutual funds we have not only the security of experts looking after our dollars all day, ever day, but our dollars are diversified over a large variety of holdings. By law, a mutual fund can not invest more than 5% of its total dollars into any one investment; nor can it own more than 10% of any one industry. As a result, a fund has as few as twenty to as many as several hundred investments in its portfolio. And, even if you invest only $100 you own a portion of all those companies, because in effect, you own a portion of that fund.

I love it. I think you should too.

# Full time professionals

Do you know anything about the inside of your TV set? Chances are you don't. Somebody a lot more knowledgeable than you and I in the field of electronics, spent days, weeks, months and years in developing the right tubes, coils, resistors, transistors and whatever, and put them all together in proper order and sequence. All you and I have to do is flick the switch and sit back and enjoy the results. Basically, that is what a mutual fund is. It is a component of parts (stocks, bonds, interest earning investments) put together by experts, and all you and I have to do is 'make the investment' (be it a monthly savings plan, lump sum, RRSP or whatever) and sit back and enjoy the results.

An extra advantage is the fact that our investment is under full-time day-by-day scrutiny by top experts, and if they see an investment that is no longer performing as it should, they pull it out and replace it...or add additional investments to improve performance.

Does it make sense to go to a doctor if you are sick? To a dentist with tooth problems; a mechanic with your car; a lawyer with legal problems; a tax expert, etc.? I think all of us would agree it does make sense. Then doesn't it make sense to go to an 'expert' and have that person look after your savings?

That is simply what a mutual fund is. It is 'experts' looking after your savings. Not only yours, but your neighbour's, the person's across the street, my savings, and many others in your community and across this land. We all put our savings into 'one pot' and like we enjoy TV, sit back and enjoy the results.

Most of the mutual funds available are called equity funds, although there are Income Funds (bonds and interest earning vehicles), Mortgage Funds, Real Estate Funds, Resource Funds, Gold Funds, etc. Ninety percent of the time equity funds are in stocks (businesses), because the 'experts' believe that is the best place to achieve safety and above average gain. But, if they felt the equity market was a poor place to be, or a downward trend might be coming, I've seen funds be as much as 50 percent and 60 percent in cash (earning interest). When they were largely cash could we say they were a stock fund? Certainly not.

You may prefer funds which invest in bonds, or mortgages, or real estate, or speculative issues, oil and gas, energy, or the broad spectrum of all of those. You may prefer funds that invest primarily in Canadian holdings, or others that invest worldwide, so that you share in the economies and growth of many different nations. We've seen funds that primarily invested in Canada, then shifted for several years to European investments such as Germany, England, then move to Japanese investments, and eventually to U.S. investments and now into the far east and even Latin America. The investor who placed his savings into such a fund and left them there for 20 years has shared in the economic growth of all those lands during their boom periods, and he never had to make a move or a decision. Where else can you make an investment like that? A typical example is Templeton Growth Fund, which has invested in all those countries at differing times, and where in the past 40 years an investment of $1000 would now be worth over $300,000. ($1000 at 12% compounded would become $93,000 over the same period.)

Mutual funds have been in Canada now for over 60 years. For several years the term 'investment funds' has also been used. Both terms are used extensively when describing this type of investment.

Various magazine and newspaper articles are now beginning to recognize this method of investing. Why is this?

We believe this overdue acceptance by money management writers is because mutual funds have proven to be one of the safest and most prof-itable ways of allowing Canadians to share in the profit of their country's growth. Their performance is published daily in most city newspapers and their past performance is regularly compared in the financial papers.

These results, when examined regularly, will show which are good performers and which are average. Comparing them to a 'normal' investment, the average mutual fund gain is double, and the good mutual fund gain would show to be triple. We think the difference comes back to the professional management aspect of all funds. Just as there are excellent car mechanics, a lot of good ones, and even some poor ones, so it is in the investment business. This is why we believe it is advantageous, when looking to start investing in a mutual fund, you seek out the advice of an independent representative. Someone who has no loyalty to any one fund, but rather has as a first loyalty, you, the investor. Your needs will be different than those of others. The independent advisor will act on your behalf to match the type of funds to your particular financial goals.

# Which funds are excellent?

Fortunately, there are three financial papers in Canada which report mutual fund performance statistics regularly. *The Financial Times* of Canada produces monthly tables showing the average percentage rate of return for the previous one year, three years, five years, and ten years. the *Financial*

*Post* and *Globe and Mail* produces similar statistics, showing the total gain over the past one, five, and ten years. These statistics on well over 700 mutual funds, give you an indication of what each of those funds was able to do in relation to all the other funds during the same time span.

Because of the diversification of all funds the good performers (relative to each other) can be attributed not so much to the market itself, but to the managers of those higher performing funds. However, none of the statistics disclose any possible change in management, or for that matter who was responsible for the fund's achievement.

This is why we feel it is wise to consult with an independent mutual fund specialist who knows all the funds available, the current management picture, and the probable reasons for good or poor performance. This specialist works with no particular fund group, but rather has a variety of excellent performing funds that can be offered. Specialists know that if they don't put your money into the best funds, you will leave them and find someone who will. That is why the mutual fund specialist is constantly studying the statistics, getting to know the managers of funds, learning each of their investment philosophies, and then recommending the funds that they feel would best suit your needs and goals.

# My favourites

Today's investment world can be confusing, and so can the myriad of mutual funds. After all, today there are the most popular 'equity' funds. There are the interest-earning funds like bond funds, mortgage funds, treasury bill funds, and money market funds. There are many specialty funds that choose a portfolio of industry segments like natural resource funds, option funds, gold funds, nursing home funds, real estate funds, transportion, oil and gas, and utilities.

There are funds that confine their investment activity to Japan or Europe...or to Canada. In fact those that qualify for RRSP contributions must, by law, have 80% or more of their assets invested within Canada. There are growth funds, balanced funds and divided funds. There are funds that invest in 'bargain' stocks, there are 'gun-slinger' funds that invest in what is 'hot' today only to get out shortly for what is 'hot' tomorrow. And there are new ones all the time; but which ones to choose?

My favourites are the wide-open, conservative equity funds.

'Wide-open' means the fund can invest anywhere in the world. It can have part of the portfolio in industries, oil and gas, bank ownership,

or almost anything that holds real value and
potential for growth. The fund can switch to
interest-earning investments if the managers feel
there will be a prolonged 'down' in the market.

'Conservative' means the funds' money is
invested in only sound, proven industries, not newly
emerged ones or such things as mines. I'm not smart
enough to know what is sound or has potential, so I
trust my investments to the fund managers who are
conservative. I let them make the choices and let
them watch over those choices. It's the ideal way to
invest.

# Equal treatment

Where can Mr. and Mrs. Average Canadian
be treated to the same results as the person with
several million dollars? In mutual funds, of course.
You see in a mutual fund, over the same time span,
everyone achieves exactly the same rate of return as
everyone else. No one in the fund can achieve more
gain...or less gain. Mutual funds usually calculate
their values every day. The exception is some trust
company funds which calculate only once a week or
once a month. Everyone who buys on a certain day,
purchases units or shares at the same value. The

same is true at the time of sale. The fund has no
choice but to redeem shares or units for you, at the
price calculated on the day of your redemption
request. Whether you have $1000 or $1,000,000, you
get the same treatment when buying and selling.
And everyone enjoys the same rate of return.

# Long-term investment

Maybe your definition is different than mine,
but when I say long-term, I mean a minimum of five
years. Many of us have 'locked-up' our money in
5-year Term Deposits, G.I.C.'s, or 5-to-25 year
mortgages.

Because economies and their ups and downs
tend to run in cycles I like to examine the past
performance of a fund in 15-year time spans. In
looking at the last 29-year history of one fund, the
Templeton Growth Fund, we can see sixteen
15-year spans between 1964 and 1993 inclusive.

## Compounded Annual Average *Change*

| | | | | |
|---|---|---|---|---|
| 1964 | +28.40% | | 1979 | +24.50% |
| 1965 | +22.00% | | 1980 | +26.80% |
| 1966 | - 5.20% | | 1981 | - 0.90% |
| 1967 | +13.31% | | 1982 | +15.00% |
| 1968 | +36.51% | | 1983 | +34.50% |
| 1969 | +19.91% | | 1984 | + 8.60% |
| 1970 | -11.83% | | 1985 | +35.10% |
| 1971 | +20.74% | | 1986 | +19.70% |
| 1972 | +67.50% | | 1987 | - 5.10% |
| 1973 | - 9.89% | | 1988 | +12.30% |
| 1974 | -12.60% | | 1989 | +21.20% |
| 1975 | +41.23% | | 1990 | -13.58% |
| 1976 | +45.05% | | 1991 | +30.30% |
| 1977 | +30.90% | | 1992 | +15.23% |
| 1978 | +29.10% | | 1993 | +36.30% |

## 15-year Compounded Average Annual *Result*

| | | | | |
|---|---|---|---|---|
| 1964-1978 | 19.0% | | 1972-1986 | 22.0% |
| 1965-1979 | 18.8% | | 1973-1987 | 17.5% |
| 1966-1980 | 19.2% | | 1974-1988 | 19.2% |
| 1967-1981 | 19.4% | | 1975-1989 | 21.8% |
| 1968-1982 | 19.6% | | 1976-1990 | 17.9% |
| 1969-1983 | 19.4% | | 1977-1991 | 17.1% |
| 1970-1984 | 18.7% | | 1978-1992 | 16.1% |
| 1971-1985 | 21.4% | | 1979-1993 | 16.47% |

## Templeton Growth Fund Returns

The difference between the lowest span gain and the highest span gain is 5.9%. The worst 15-year average is 16.1% and the best is 22.0%

Putting that into dollars it means that a $10,000 investment grew to a value of $93,633 (worst span) or $197,609 (best 15-year span). See the full table on pages 174 and 175.

In 1979 your $10,000 investment at 10% interest over 15 years would have become $41,772, or at 12% would have become $54,735. Yet, the worst period for the mutual fund realized $93,633. People who invest in mutual funds should look on them as long-term investments.

Look at the table on page 178 and we find that the fund made money in 23 of the past 30 years. In 1972 the fund made a one year gain of 67%. However, there were seven years in which that fund lost money. The worst was a 13.6% loss in 1990. In 1981 the loss was a minimal .9%. Except for one instance the loss years were separated by at least two good 'gain years'. What about the double loss years of 1973 and 1974?

Let's look at the poor investor who invested just before those difficult years. If that person had an invested value of $45,376 on December 31, 1972 and left those dollars there during the two loss years, they would have seen their value decline to $40,894 by the end of 1973, and then to $35,758 by the end of 1974. What would you have done?

If you would have 'cashed out' or 'bailed out' then you would have joined the ranks of those who treat mutual funds as a short-term investment. Some of them end up as losers. On the other hand, if you had treated that investment in a similar fashion as a 5-year mortgage, G.I.C., or term deposit, you would have seen that value of $35,758 grow in 1975 to over $50,000, then to $73,260 in 1976 and to $95,931 by the end of 1977. Yes, it more than doubled in five years, despite the fact it had declined in the first two years.

That would have been one of the worst 5-year examples. The investor who was either smart or lucky enough to invest after the declines of 1973 and 1974 would have seen an investment of $35,758 average over 33% per year in the next five years to a value of over $154,500. Yes, you can lose if you only look at the short term picture.

# The up and down cycle

I read somewhere years ago, something that has stuck with me. "The market place is like a yo-yo in the hands of a man climbing stairs. Unfortunately, most of us watch only the yo-yo and forget he's climbing stairs."

It is very true, the stock market has its ups and downs. History tells us there is an average of three years up and one year down in a four year cycle. The two down years just discussed (1973 and

1974) were followed by six rather fantastic 'up years'. The average was maintained; three up to one down.

The market has always averaged up, despite the fact there are ups and downs in that average. Just like the yo-yo going up and down while the man is climbing the stairs. It pays to keep your eye on where the man is on the stairs, not on whether the yo-yo is spinning downward or upward. Despite the yo-yo effect, good mutual funds have proven to keep climbing.

# Dollar cost averaging

Here is a sure way to beat those 'ups and downs'. People always want a way to beat the market and you'll find this system mentioned in almost any book you read on how to improve your finances.

Did you know that if you invested $100 monthly in an investment that had a steady market rise that finally doubled after ten years, that you would be worth $17,250 at the end of those ten years? See the table on page 181.

If, however, the values went up and down, just as the market does, the result would be quite different. Suppose the share values in the first year are $5.00, the second year $3.00, 3rd year $6.00, 4th year $4.00, etc. finally ending up double at $10.00 in year 10. Your value would be over $22,000.

That's almost $5,000 more. The same amount was invested ($100 a month – $1,200 a year) and the stock increase was the same (doubled). By investing regularly the same amount of money, the purchaser was sometimes buying bargains at $3.00 and $4.00, and this is what gave the extra gain. Every time the share value went down, your $100 was buying more and more shares, so that when the price went back up, your increase was on the additional volume of shares. Had the value of our shares dropped from $5.00 to $4.00, to $3.00, to $2.00, and then to $1.00 during the first five years, then risen over the last five years to what you paid originally, that is $5.00, you would end up with a total value of $25,455. That's $8,000 more than if the shares had steadily increased over the same period that you invested your $100 a month. Dollar cost averaging always beats the market, if you give it time. Are you practising this principle in your savings?

The same theory would work wonders for your RRSP, too. Toward the end of February each year, we see intelligent businessmen, accountants, lawyers, doctors, dentists and lots of hard working citizens, make their tax-sheltered RRSP contribution...for the previous year. Sure, they get the tax deduction for that year, but look how they lose.

Look at the charts on pages 180 and 181. Both Mr. A and Mr. B put the maximum allowed annually into a mutual fund called Industrial Growth Fund. Mr. A put his into the RRSP each December. Mr. B, however, puts $\frac{1}{12}$ th of the annual amount every month into his RRSP. Both invest the same amount into the same fund. At the end of 25 years each had invested a total of $157,500. Mr. A would be worth $1,013,926, and Mr. B's value in the same fund would be $1,059,624.

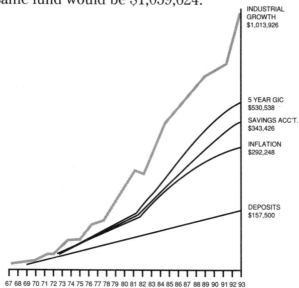

INDUSTRIAL
GROWTH
$1,013,926

5 YEAR GIC
$530,538

SAVINGS ACC'T.
$343,426

INFLATION
$292,248

DEPOSITS
$157,500

67 68 69 70 71 72 73 74 75 76 77 78 79 80 81 82 83 84 85 86 87 88 89 90 91 92 93

**Registered Retirement Savings Plan — Mr. A**

That's over $46,000 more. Mr. B knew the value of dollar cost averaging to gain the additional $46,000. By the way, a Mr. C put his RRSP dollars annually in a fixed-return 5-year G.I.C., and came out after the same period with a total of $552,420. which is $500,000 less than the mutual fund result. If you can't trust yourself to make this monthly contribution, ask your fund consultant about a Pre-Authorized Cheque plan that will automatically debit your bank or trust company account the monthly amount you wish to contribute.

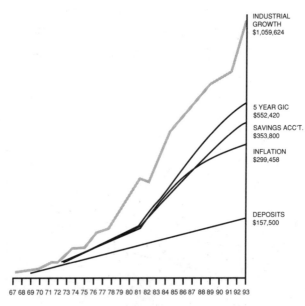

INDUSTRIAL GROWTH $1,059,624

5 YEAR GIC $552,420

SAVINGS ACC'T. $353,800

INFLATION $299,458

DEPOSITS $157,500

67 68 69 70 71 72 73 74 75 76 77 78 79 80 81 82 83 84 85 86 87 88 89 90 91 92 93

**Registered Retirement Savings Plan — Mr. B**

**5**

# Retirement

# Your retirement years

I'd like to share a true story about two senior citizens. When I first met them in 1963, they were both in their late 60's, recently widowed, and owning few assets. Let's call them Mrs. W. and Mrs. S.

Mrs. W. was left with only 25 shares of Bell Telephone and around $10,000 locked up in 5-year GIC's at different trust companies. As the certificates came due, taking my advice, Mrs. W. invested in mutual funds. Ultimately they were all invested. She held on to the Bell shares for sentimental reasons, because they paid a dividend every three months, and it was the only stock her husband had ever bought.

Mrs. S. took advice from her son and others. She was told because of her age she should stick to 'guarantees' and not risk her money in mutual funds. As they both neared 80 they found it difficult to pay for lawn mowing and snow shovelling. So they each sold their homes and, being friends, moved into a new Senior Citizens apartment side by side.

They each got about $40,000 for their homes. Mrs. W. paid the sales commission and asked me to pick up a cheque for the balance and to add it to the mutual fund investments she already had working for her. When I went, I talked to Mrs. S., but she had decided to "invest her house money where it was guaranteed".

Since each of them had to now pay rent, I was able to put Mrs. W. on an automatic withdrawal plan of $300 a month to cover her rent. Mrs. S. had to rely on the interest from 'guarantees' to pay her rent. We discovered something else. Mrs. W. qualified for the 'old age supplement', whereas Mrs. S. didn't. Mrs. S. had over $50,000 in GIC's earning 7%. Because her annual income was $3500 she got no supplement.

I helped Mrs. W. apply for her supplement each year. Although she was getting $3600 annually on the withdrawal plan, it was made up of dividends, capital gains, and withdrawal of principal. Very little of it was considered earned income, so she was able to get a supplement from the government of between $60 and $70 every month.

Mrs. S., having to live on less and less, because her principal was being eroded, died almost destitute. Mrs. W. spent the last several years of her life in a nursing home, requiring a larger monthly withdrawal of $600 from her funds. She died at the age of 90 with mutual funds worth $98,000.

Two friends with the same original assets; but what a difference the "type" of investment made in their lives.

# Guarantees

Most of us are guarantee conscious. We consider a certain car because of a manufacturer's warranty or guarantee of, say, three years or 60,000 kilometres. We buy a particular appliance because is is guaranteed to operate for two years without any problems. We invest in Guaranteed Certificates because they are guaranteed. Thanks to the Canada Deposit Corporation, if the issuing bank or trust company were to go bankrupt, we are guaranteed to get our money back up to $60,000. (We are not guaranteed to keep receiving the interest from the bankrupt savings institution.)

Most of our parents instilled this principle into us. I know my dad taught me to be very cautious with my savings. To always seek out guarantees. That was fine for the times...back in the 30's and 40's. Then there was no inflation and my dad paid no income tax. But times have changed and maybe a guarantee for our savings isn't all it's supposed to be.

Remember there is no such thing as a riskless investment, just degrees and types of risks. Those fixed-income investments, sold as guaranteed certificates, are always subject to purchasing power risk. If you fix your rate of return for a fixed period, and interest rates were to rise, too bad, because you will continue to get the lower rate. If interest rates

were to decline, you earn at the better fixed rate,
but only for the fixed term. When your term investment came due, on re-investmentent you would
have to accept the lower rate. On top of those 'risks'
comes the *greater* risk of taxation and its erosion on
your real income. If you look at the Tables in the
appendix you will see the evidence that an investor
in interest-earning 'investments' could actually lose
purchasing power (thanks to inflation and taxation)
over a ten year period by earning interest.

# Gambling with inflation

They say older people shouldn't gamble with
their money. Venita Van Caspel, in her book, 'Power
of Money Dynamics', says the real gamblers are
those who invest in 'guarantees'. She reasons, that
with the fixed income produced by the 'guarantees',
you are gambling that the twin evils of taxation and
inflation will not erode away all your gain. Many
mutual funds, although never guaranteed, have a
proven performance of more than 15% over the last
10 years.

# Your nest egg

Suppose your are 45, your kids are now working and the house is nearly paid for, and now you want to start saving. You put $4,000 a year into a regular RRSP or savings program at 15% average annual gain. At 65 you will have a value of $471,000. If inflation were to average 5.89% (that's the average over the past 30 years) over those 20 years, you would need $80,170 annual income to match $25,000 today. Then, if your nest egg were to earn 10% annually from age 65 onward, your annual income from it would be $47,100. You would be short $33,000 per year of spending power that you're used to today.

I hope these figures scare you. They can't be changed; they are simple mathematics. To make your leisure years worry free, start now to plan your retirement.

# Winners and inflation

Let's follow four case histories

Mr. B followed the advice of virtually every advisor and put his $100,000 in to a 10% interest earning investment. Mr. A put his $100,000 into a mutual fund called Industrial Growth Fund. Both decided to take an income of $9,000 a year from their investment returns. Thanks to income taxes, Mr. B. only had $6,500 left to spend, because his return was fully taxable. Mr. A. had over $8,000 to spend, because his income was made up from return of principal, dividends, and capital gains (which are minimally taxed). Each year, as inflation eroded the $9,000 return, they increased their income to match inflation. After 26 years, just to keep up with inflation they each needed $43,321 in 1993. But poor Mr. B. (10% investor) was hypothetically $377,901 in the hole, because his fixed return of 10% couldn't keep up. Lucky Mr. A. continued to receive his inflation indexed return AND he had $418,144 left invested. (See the full table on page 172.)

Now, Mr. C., who invested the same $100,000, but four years earlier, in a 10% fixed return investment, needed $48,516 / 30 years later to match the inflated $9,000. He was (if he could be) $461,053 in the hole, Mr. D., after thirty years of a $100,000 investment in the Templeton Growth Fund, had not only received an inflation indexed income each year, but had over $3,400,000 left in the fund. See the full table on page 173.

Who was the big winner?

# The indexed pension

We certainly don't want to go in the hole, meaning lose our money. But when we try to retire on a fixed income, that's what happens, no matter how large it is.

There is a way to beat this inflation spiral. It's the withdrawal plan offered by many different mutual funds. Only once in my 32 years in the mutual fund business, have I seen a writer explain or even know about this fantastic program.

# The withdrawal plan

How does it work? And how can it give an almost tax-free income to the investor? Let me use another illustration to show you how it works.

Suppose you purchase a 100 acre farm for $1,000 an acre. It then goes up in value to $1,100 an acre. It is now worth $110,000.

You decide to sell off nine acres (representing 9% of your holdings) at the $1,100 price. This puts

$9,900 in your pocket. The first $9,000 is completely tax-free because it's a return of your own money. The balance of $900, represents a capital gain of $100 an acre. Under the Capital Gains holiday proclaimed in the May 1985 budget, there would be no tax whatsoever. If the $100,000 tax-free capital gains holiday had been used up (or cancelled by the Government) 75% of this $900 capital gain would be taxable. Therefore the $675 would be taxable, if in the 50% tax bracket, it would cost you no more than $338 in tax. So, of the $9,900 you received, you have $9,562 left to spend. Further-more, the value of your remaining 91 acres is $100,100 ($110,000 minus $9,900). And...we haven't even considered that in addition – if you are a good farmer – you will also have a profit (earnings) in addition to your increased values.

This is still more than you paid for the farm. True, you may have less acreage, but your value has been maintained while you have drawn off 9% of your original investment.

It works the same with a mutual fund. You purchase so many shares or units for your $100,000 investment and draw off each year, or month, a certain percentage as income. If it were 9% the first year (based on the same 10% increased value to $110,000) you would get $825 a month (or $9,900). As your investment grew by 12% or 15%, you would maybe increase your withdrawal to 10% or 13%, without ever touching your original capital investment. That's how you can keep ahead of inflation. And you don't need $100,000 for a withdrawal plan. You can start a monthly withdrawal plan with only $5,000. The details are all looked after by your chosen mutual fund office and the payments are then automatic.

Incidentally, if you have put your $100,000 into a fixed income investment with a return of 10% interest (meaning $10,000 a year) you would have to pay tax on the full amount. If you were in the 50% tax bracket you would only have $5,000 left to spend each year. Which would you rather have to spend, $5,000 or $9,562? Also, the interest bearing investment can never grow beyond the original $100,000

# My 'secret' formula

Others are now talking about it, but for a long while nobody could understand how simple it was. You see, with the withdrawal plan, you can be completely flexible. Since you're not locked into any fixed return, you can change, increase or decrease your income at any time. Experience has shown that good mutual funds, over the past decades, have averaged 15% and better. This allows you to withdraw a good income (remember it's almost tax-free) and still have it come from a larger and larger amount, as it continues to grow. Do you know of a better investment for those who can no longer work for a living? Most of us will live a long time into retirement. Will you and your loved one be able to maintain your standard of living?

# Should I buy an annuity?

Almost every one nearing retirement talks about the time they will live off their annuity. Even younger people are sold RRSP's and insurance policies with the idea that they can convert those mature dollars into an annuity and 'live happily ever after'. In most cases, we believe an annuity is not the answer for retirement years.

To put it simply, an annuity is the exchange of a lump sum of money for a fixed monthly income. Almost all annuities are 'life' plans. They guarantee a regular income for as long as you live. In addition some people take a term guarantee of say 10 or 15 years, so that if death occurred, the income would continue into the estate for the given period. If you take a guarantee, however, the monthly payout is much less than the straight life annuity.

There are two guarantees that the prospective purchaser should know about.

Most annuity merchants will never talk about them. The first unrevealed guarantee is that the purchaser will have to live on less and less because of inflation. It's not the fault of the annuity, but once the monthly payment figure has been set, that's all you will have to live on. The second uninterpreted guarantee is that after the guarantee period is over, or the annuitant has died (whichever is later), you are guaranteed to have nothing left. Nothing goes to your estate for your family. That's guaranteed.

# Don't listen to your children

A few years ago a Sarnia woman in her late 80's, who had frugally managed to save $100,000, was approached by an insurance salesman. He convinced her to put her savings into a life annuity which would guarantee her a monthly income for as long as she lived. Her three children were also convinced that she was doing the right thing.

But 'Mom' made a fortunate phone call to an independent investment consultant and told him of her plan to purchase an annuity that afternoon. The consultant had other appointments, but cancelled them and drove to Sarnia. He pointed out that at her age she probably could not get a guaranteed period and therefore the life annuity would leave nothing to her children after her death. When the children were called in from their respective homes, they did not believe there would be no money left when 'Mom' died. The consultant challenged them to get a letter of guarantee from the agent that there would be something left. His response was "Our company doesn't give such guarantees".

Ultimately the elderly woman invested those dollars into a mutual fund instead of the annuity. She immediately took out a monthly income that was equal to what the annuity would have paid. She received this amount for the next four years. After she died the three children shared in the more than $100,000 that was still remaining in the fund.

# The annuity contract

In another case, a businessman who had taken out life insurance to ensure his wife would have sufficient funds to buy-out his portion of the company, died at the early age of 41. The insurance company was prompt in paying the proceeds of the policy and had the agent, within two weeks, deliver the cheque. Unfortunately, the story didn't end there.

The insurance agent was 'very helpful' and assured the widow that if she signed the papers he had brought, she would be comfortably set for the rest of her life. Being upset from the death of her husband, she signed the papers. She signed to purchase a life annuity.

The other partners in her husbands business enquired if she was going to pay off her portion of the business bank loan. She couldn't because she had signed the papers for the annuity. Even her lawyer was unable to reverse the annuity contract. She was unable to save her deceased husband's portion of the business.

# What about my RRSP conversion?

The government says we must convert our tax-protected RRSP dollars into income before the end of the year in which we turn 71. We have learned from the previous examples, that an annuity is not our recommended tool for this purpose. There is another option called a Registered Retirement Income Fund (RRIF). Legislation was passed in 1986 that allows a RRIF owner to take an income of any amount desired (subject to a very small minimum) and can increase or decrease that income any time so chosen. You can also have more than one RRIF, or transfer the RRIF from one carrier to another. If the purchaser should die the payments or the value remaining (if any) would go to the estate. With a RRIF you also have a measure of control on how your money is invested. You can change to an investment that achieves greater safety or greater gain, or change the payment formula to suit your needs. With the ability to increase your payments, the RRIF can probably keep you ahead of inflation. At least, you'll have choice, flexibility and control.

# Control your assets

Another recommended option is to withdraw your RRSP assets piece by piece beginning at age 65. You will pay tax on it, but you are freeing up some capital for investments over which you will have complete control. Here's how it works.

At age 65 you retire with $70,000 in your RRSP. The first year you de-register one seventh of the value and include the $10,000 in your taxable income. The next year you de-register one sixth, that with growth will probably yield $11,000. At age 67 you de-register one fifth, and so on, until the year you turn 71 when all the money has been freed up. If you would put the converted dollars into mutual funds, you could take, say, a monthly withdrawal of $700 and if inflation dictated or you needed money for a vacation, you could increase your income. You control it during your lifetime. And, past performance has shown, you will still be able to leave an estate approximating the original value of your RRSP.

# How do I become a millionaire?

I don't believe there is any secret to achieving wealth. It simply entails saving a part of what you earn and leaving those savings to grow and compound.

Suppose you are 25 years old and earn $8.00 an hour. For a 40 hour week that's $320. If you were to save 10% of what you earn, that would be $32 a week, or $1,664 a year. If you invest that money at a rate of 15% per year, and allow those dollars to compound, you would be worth $1,686,000 at age 60 and $3,400,000 at age 65.

If you were smart enough to start saving at age 25, you would also be smart enough to know how to borrow money. And after saving the first $5,000 you would use other peoples' money (borrowed) to invest and earn even more profits. You the smart person could end up with $10 or $20 million by age 65. And remember at age 25 you were only earning $8.00 an hour.

Why do we resist borrowing in order to invest? We probably borrowed to buy our car. And we undoubtedly borrowed (took out a mortgage) to buy our home. We used Other Peoples' Money

(O.P.M.). Take that home of yours. If you borrowed $20,000 to pay for it 30 years ago and find that today it's worth over $100,000, you have gained $80,000 using O.P.M. You could do more than that.

Suppose you could borrow $20,000 from your bank (a mortgage collateral loan) at let's say 12% interest. Because the interest costs are tax deductible, it means that, if you are in the 40% tax – (median) bracket, your real cost is 7.2%. Now you could invest that $20,000 into a mutual fund that conservatively averages you 15% annually, meaning a net profit of 7.8%. This gain bears very little taxation, because it is made up of capital gains and dividends. The 7.8% net profit amounts to $1,560 a year that your house earns for you.

# The tax-deductible mortgage

The longer we own a house, the easier the payments usually become. We continue paying the mortgage, month after month, with no tax benefit.

After 35 years of living in my house, I still haven't paid for it. You see, I have it mortgaged to the maximum amount. And I have the borrowed money invested in mutual funds. Here's how it works.

I tell my kids that it costs us $18,000 a year to live in our house. The taxes are over $3,000. The fuel costs are almost $1,000 some winters. And the water, hydro, repairs and maintenance run about another $2,000.

Well that's $6,000. Where's the other $12,000 go? The $12,000 is what I could be making if the money the house is worth were invested instead of in bricks and stone. For simplification, my house is worth $150,000 and if that were earning interest at 10% I'd be getting $15,000 return. But I don't have that money. I have the house instead. So what do I do? I use the house as collateral to borrow $100,000 from the bank.

Suppose my mortgage is 12% and I'm in the 50% tax bracket. Since the borrowed money is re-invested, the mortgage costs are tax deductible. That means the money costs, after tax, only 6%. The return on my investments in mutual funds has been between 15% and 20% over the last 30 years. But these earnings are capital gains and dividends which bear very little tax. Let's say I only made 15% and lost 3% to taxes. My after-tax gain is 12%, which cost me 6% (true mortgage cost after tax deduction). The restult is a 6% GAIN. That means a $100,000 mortgage on my house can EARN me – not COST me – $6,000 a year.

Actually, I leave the investments and the house loan at the bank, as security, and borrow another $200,000. This gives me $18,000 gain on the $300,000 borrowed and re-invested. Now my house gives me free living. It also earns me an income. My payments at the bank are covered by a withdrawal plan directly to the bank to pay the interest...and thanks to inflation my house is now valued at over $300,000.

# It takes money to make money

Most of us know the saying, but few of us employ it in our lives. I didn't always have a lot of money working for me. I started over 30 years ago by borrowing. Of course I had to *save first*. But, after taking a little out of my pay each week I had $5,000 saved. Then I borrowed another $5,000 from the bank. I had my first O.P.M. working for me. Today that $5,000 loan has grown to over $1 million. And...I look forward to the day it will be $2 million.

# More $$$ from less

It is possible to use less dollars in the same investment over the same period of time and end up with more dollars. It's based on three fundamental investment rules: 1) take advantage of the tax laws, 2) use other people's money, and 3) make the time factor work for you.

Two men decided they could invest $100 monthly into a mutual fund called Cundill Value Fund. Mr. Saver took the money out of his income and at the end of 19 years he had invested a total of $22,900. At the end of the 19 years he was worth over $132,305. (In a bank account at 10% it would be worth close to $69,000).

Mr. Borrower, on the other hand, went to the bank and borrowed $10,000 outright and put the total into the fund. His interest payments were 12% a year, or $100 a month. At the end of the same 19 years he was worth $264,947. He had paid a total of $22,900 in interest ($100 a month) and he now paid back the $10,000 loan, leaving him with $254,947. That's $122,000 more than Mr. Saver.

You are now going to remind me that I promised the big earner would actually have invested less. Well, it's true. Mr. Borrower, being in the 40% tax bracket, and having invested his loan, was able to deduct that portion of his $100 monthly interest payments ($100 – 40% = $60 true cost) on his tax return. Rather than $22,800, his true cost over the 19 years was only $13,680 (the other $5,040 was a tax saving).

Less money invested (Government paid $9,120...you paid $13,680)...into the same fund...over the same period...but with more results. The difference here is *time*. The $10,000 worked for the whole 19 years, whereas only the first $100 worked for 19 years, the second. $100 for 18 years and 11 months, etc. etc,; the last $100 investment having worked for only one month.

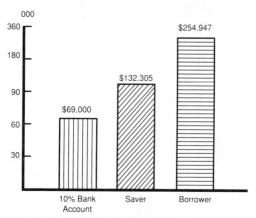

**Investment of $100 per month
for 19 years**

# What's it worth?

Everyone wants to know what it costs. Like a lot of other things the fee structure depends on what and how much you are purchasing. For instance, there are some 'no-load' mutual funds. That means there is no fee for the purchase of shares in those funds.

There are many more 'load' mutual funds. These charge a fee, depending on the amount invested, from 3% to 9%. When you pay an acquisition fee to purchase a fund, you are paying for the services provided by the representative. You are availing yourself of his knowledge and expertise. Chances are, that if he is an independent agent, representing dozens of mutual funds, he would recommend only those funds which he felt would perform according to your particular financial goals. Chances are that he will sit down with you and spend several hours, in one or two visits maybe, to work out your present financial position, what your future position would be after accepting the recommendations.

Chances are a complete financial program would be laid out for you to consider, to accept or reject. Ways and means to reduce the bite of income taxes would be explained. RRSP's and RRIF's would be explained. Ideas on how to reduce the committed cost of your house by up to 40% would be available.

The representative would try to keep you and your investments in the top producing funds, because if he doesn't you would probably find someone else who would. For the additional safety factor, however, he would probably suggest a portfolio of several different funds, under different managers.

And now, you can purchase funds with no up-front fee. There is something called a Deferred Sales Charge (DSC) option whereby there is no cost to invest, but there is an exit (or redemption) fee if you get out early. This fee is a declining fee, as an example, if you redeemed in the first year it might be 5%, in the second year 4%, in the third year 3%, etc. In many funds the fee disappears down to 0% exit fee after five years, although there are some where it takes 9 years to get to 0%.

# On-going service

You would continue to get on-going service, in a regular review of your investment situation, and in continuing suggestions for your financial improvement. These and many other services come with the representative's attention to your account. You can accept or reject his plan for your financial growth. Only when you accept the purchase recommendation, does the fee apply.

# On your own

Should you not want these advisory services, you can take the time yourself to study statistics, do your research, on your own. You may seek out a no-load fund and decide to participate. You will be bombarded with literature and reports. You will be given suggestions to add to your investments, but you will have no independent, objective voice to discuss the alternatives with.

You may wish to compare past performance over a ten-year period between no-load and load funds. I could give you figures to look at from both kinds of funds, but these records you may wish to discover for yourself.

# Does the fund manager get paid?

When it comes to putting our savings to work, we should turn to a professional, the person who knows about investing. A person who spends his or her full time studying when and what to do. These professionals are not bankers. Bankers spend their day lending out money at a high rate. Or trying to borrow your money at a lower rate. Neither are lawyers experts at investing.

The real experts, who spend each full day looking at how and where to invest best, and whose performance record is on public view, are the managers of mutual funds. If they are not good at their job they will be replaced before people start moving their investments to other funds.

They do earn top salaries, and they are worth it. On our own we could not afford this expense. But shared with the hundreds of thousands of mutual fund owners, it becomes minimal.

In a mutual fund a small investor of $1,000 joins with a millionaire in paying for the constant management of the funds welfare. In the Templeton Group of Funds, for example, there are now many millions of shareholders. The management fee, assessed to the fund annually, is between .5% and 2%. Even at 2% it costs me only $20 a year to have an expert look after my investment. That's less than 6¢ a day. Do you know of any financial expert that will work for you for 6¢ a day?

# 6

# Conclusion

Conclusion

# Your short term desires

Most of us share the same goals in life: some day to retire with dignity and wealth; to really enjoy life; to travel and entertain. But, because it's a long range goal, we tend to forget it, or ignore it.

We are much happier meeting our short term goals by spending our extra money on things we desire rather than need. After all, we could use a new car, new drapes, or perhaps an addition to the house, like a new bathroom.

If these items are needed, they should be paid for with some other dollars, not your saving dollars. Don't destroy your future retirement and those long term goals by dipping into your savings. It will cost you a lot more than you think.

I have saved this story to the end because it illustrates how I feel we should all think and act in regards to our saving versus spending. It is also a popular anecdote that has brought me a lot of response from the enquiring media.

# The $334,000 car

At the age of 30 an acquaintance of mine decided to save $100 a month. He did so quite diligently until he was 45 years old. Because he had invested in mutual funds that had averaged 15% return each year for the fifteen years, he now had an accumulated value of $61,736. He was naturally quite pleased with this balance. However, he was equally pleased with his new young bride and decided to buy her a car of her own. He took out $10,000 from his nest-egg to make the purchase.

When I heard about it I was quick to tell him that he had really spent $163,365 on the shiny new coupe. He had lost sight of his future retirement. It was still 20 years away, so why worry. But he should not have touched or interrupted that plan of investing. Here's how I explained the real cost of that car to him.

If that $10,000 had remained invested for the remaining 20 years at 15% it would have grown, at his retirement to $163,365. That amount of money would provide an income at 12% of $1,633.65 a month or $19,639.00 a year. That's almost $20,000 income per year lost forever.

They tell us that if a male lives to age 65, he will live an average of another 17 years. So the loss for the average male, going into retirement, would now be $333,863. By losing a potential annual income of $19,639 a year for 17 years, the loss amounts to over a THIRD OF A MILLION DOLLARS!

That proved to be a rather expensive car. So, my advice is to not substitute short term desires for your long term goals. If you do, it could prove to be very costly.

# The best!

We all strive to be the best.

Our Olympic Athletes work and practise for years in an effort to be best. To win the coveted Gold award. Winning it proves for the rest of their lives they were the best. Our sports teams, be they hockey, baseball, football, or basketball, all strive to be the best and win the cup or pennant. Individuals in the field of tennis or golf also strive to be the best.

Is there a best investment that should win an award? Is there something that over time has proven again and again to be up there at the top? I believe there is.

I cast my vote for the best investment. Mutual Funds!

Sure I'm prejudiced, after living in the industry for 32 years. But...having done so, and having seen the results that have occurred for virtually everyone who has treated them as a long-term investment, I am even more convinced. Having told hundreds, yes thousands of people, the mutual fund story, I've asked again and again: "Do you know of a better investment than this?" Not one has told me they know of a better investment.

# Nothing better

I've gone even further and told people, "If you know of a better investment than mutual funds, then please do two things.
1.  Invest your dollars there, and
2.  Let me know the investment that is better, so that I can invest also."

Not one, no, not one person, has shared with me an investment they believe to be better. If there is a better way to save and invest, perhaps people want to keep it a secret and not share it with others.

Because no one knows of, or will tell me there are better investments, I've arrived at the logical conclusion that mutual funds are indeed the best way to save and invest your dollars. In fact, I believe history has proven it.

Admittedly, there are all kinds of single investments that have proven to be fantastic. The people who invested with the inventor of the game 'Trivial Pursuit' have all become millionaires. Others who invested in the 'right' company at the 'right' time may have done better. Or, those who invested in a mine, or oil well that became a producer, may have done well. But all of those items required study, time, and maybe even a little bit of luck. Also, many 'booms' just lasted a short time, and then petered out.

Mutual funds have been in Canada for over 60 years, and many have proven records over 10-year periods of averaging 15% or better per year. That means you double your money every five years.

They're fantastic! I think mutual funds are the best!

**7**

# Appendix

# Money Management Forms

## Net worth statement

Date _____

| Assets | | Liabilities | |
|---|---|---|---|
| **Assets** | | **Liabilities** | |
| Bank Accounts | _____ | Bank Loans | _____ |
| | _____ | | _____ |
| | _____ | | _____ |
| Bonds & | _____ | Outstanding | _____ |
| Certificates | _____ | Contracts | _____ |
| | _____ | | _____ |
| Stocks & | _____ | Mortgages | _____ |
| Securities | _____ | | _____ |
| Mutual Funds | _____ | Taxes Owed | _____ |
| | | | _____ |
| Life | _____ | Household | _____ |
| Insurance | _____ | Bills | _____ |
| (Cash Value) | _____ | | _____ |
| Profit Sharing | _____ | Other debts | _____ |
| Retirement | _____ | | _____ |
| Plan | _____ | | _____ |
| R.R.S.P. | _____ | | _____ |
| Real Estate | _____ | | |
| Automobile | _____ | **Total Debts** | _____ |
| Value | | | |
| Household | _____ | | |
| Goods | | | |
| Other Assets | _____ | | |
| **Total Assets** | _____ | **Net Worth** | _____ |

## Estimated Financial Resources

Period _____

| Income | Payment | Period Total |
|---|---|---|
| Employment | | |
|   Self | _____ | _____ |
|   Spouse | _____ | _____ |
| Government | | |
|   U.I.C. | _____ | _____ |
|   Family Allowance | _____ | _____ |
| Workman's Compensation | | |
|   Canada Pension | _____ | _____ |
|   Veteran Pension | _____ | _____ |
|   Old Age Security | _____ | _____ |
| Investments | | |
|   Bank Interest | _____ | _____ |
|   Bond Interest | _____ | _____ |
|   Dividends | _____ | _____ |
|   Net Rents | _____ | _____ |
|   Other | _____ | _____ |
| Retirement | | |
|   Pensions | _____ | _____ |
|   Annuities | _____ | _____ |
|   Other | _____ | _____ |
| Other Income | _____ | _____ |
| Savings on Account | _____ | _____ |
| Money to Borrow | _____ | _____ |
| Gifts | _____ | _____ |
| Inheritances | _____ | _____ |
| **Total** | _____ | _____ |

## Estimated Expenses

Period _____

| Fixed Expenses | Monthly | Annually |
|---|---|---|
| Rent | | |
| Mortgage | | |
| Property Taxes | | |
| Hydro | | |
| Water | | |
| Telephone Basic Charge | | |
| Property Insurance | | |
| Automobile Insurance | | |
| Health Insurance | | |
| Life Insurance | | |
| Regular Commuting | | |
| Car Licence | | |
| Tuition Fees | | |
| Charity/Church | | |
| Alimony | | |
| Instalment Payments | | |
| Savings | | |
| Investments | | |
| **Total Fixed Expenses** | | |

**Period** _____

| Fixed Expenses | Monthly | Annually |
|---|---|---|
| Groceries | | |
| Maid Service | | |
| Long Distance Telephone | | |
| Furnishings | | |
| Transportation | | |
| Gasoline | | |
| Car Maintenance | | |
| Clothing | | |
| Doctor | | |
| Dentist | | |
| Entertainment | | |
| Cigarettes | | |
| Alcohol | | |
| Athletics/Gym | | |
| Personal Needs | | |
| Dining Out | | |
| Vacations | | |
| Other | | |
| **Total Flexible Expenses** | | |
| **Total Fixed Expenses** | | |
| **Total Expenses** | | |

## The Budget Plan

Period _____

Total Resources
Expected                                    _____

Total Estimated
Expenses                        _____

Total Invested Amount           _____

Total Expenditures        –     _____

BALANCE                                      _____

# The
# Magic of
# Compounding
# Interest

## THE MAGIC OF COMPOUNDING INTEREST

If you deposit $1,000 in one lump sum and allow the interest to
accumulate, here is the value which it will increase to

| Yr | 5% | 6% | 7% | 8% | 9% | 10% |
|----|------|------|------|------|------|------|
| 1 | 1050 | 1060 | 1070 | 1080 | 1090 | 1100 |
| 2 | 1103 | 1124 | 1145 | 1166 | 1188 | 1210 |
| 3 | 1158 | 1191 | 1225 | 1260 | 1295 | 1331 |
| 4 | 1216 | 1262 | 1311 | 1360 | 1412 | 1464 |
| 5 | 1276 | 1338 | 1403 | 1469 | 1539 | 1611 |
| 6 | 1340 | 1419 | 1501 | 1587 | 1677 | 1772 |
| 7 | 1407 | 1504 | 1606 | 1714 | 1828 | 1949 |
| 8 | 1477 | 1594 | 1718 | 1851 | 1993 | 2144 |
| 9 | 1551 | 1689 | 1838 | 1999 | 2172 | 2358 |
| 10 | 1629 | 1791 | 1967 | 2159 | 2367 | 2594 |
| 11 | 1710 | 1898 | 2105 | 2332 | 2580 | 2853 |
| 12 | 1796 | 2012 | 2252 | 2518 | 2813 | 3138 |
| 13 | 1886 | 2133 | 2410 | 2720 | 3066 | 3452 |
| 14 | 1980 | 2261 | 2579 | 2937 | 3342 | 3797 |
| 15 | 2079 | 2397 | 2759 | 3172 | 3642 | 4177 |
| 16 | 2183 | 2540 | 2952 | 3426 | 3970 | 4595 |
| 17 | 2292 | 2693 | 3159 | 3700 | 4328 | 5054 |
| 18 | 2407 | 2854 | 3380 | 3996 | 4717 | 5560 |
| 19 | 2527 | 3026 | 3617 | 4316 | 5142 | 6116 |
| 20 | 2653 | 3207 | 3870 | 4661 | 5604 | 6727 |
| 21 | 2786 | 3400 | 4141 | 5034 | 6109 | 7400 |
| 22 | 2925 | 3604 | 4430 | 5437 | 6659 | 8140 |
| 23 | 3072 | 3820 | 4741 | 5871 | 7258 | 8954 |
| 24 | 3225 | 4049 | 5072 | 6341 | 7911 | 9850 |
| 25 | 3386 | 4292 | 5427 | 6848 | 8623 | 10835 |
| 26 | 3556 | 4549 | 5807 | 7396 | 9399 | 11918 |
| 27 | 3733 | 4822 | 6214 | 7988 | 10245 | 13110 |
| 28 | 3920 | 5112 | 6649 | 8627 | 11167 | 14421 |
| 29 | 4116 | 5418 | 7114 | 9317 | 12172 | 15863 |
| 30 | 4322 | 5743 | 7612 | 10063 | 13268 | 17449 |
| 31 | 4538 | 6088 | 8145 | 10868 | 14462 | 19194 |
| 32 | 4765 | 6453 | 8715 | 11737 | 15763 | 21114 |
| 33 | 5003 | 6841 | 9325 | 12676 | 17182 | 23225 |
| 34 | 5253 | 7251 | 9978 | 13690 | 18728 | 25548 |
| 35 | 5516 | 7686 | 10677 | 14785 | 20414 | 28102 |
| 36 | 5792 | 8147 | 11424 | 15968 | 22251 | 30913 |
| 37 | 6081 | 8636 | 12224 | 17246 | 24254 | 34004 |
| 38 | 6385 | 9154 | 13079 | 18625 | 26437 | 37404 |
| 39 | 6705 | 9704 | 13995 | 20115 | 28816 | 41145 |
| 40 | 7040 | 10286 | 14974 | 21725 | 31409 | 45259 |

| Yr | 11% | 12% | 13% | 14% | 15% | 16% |
|----|-----|-----|-----|-----|-----|-----|
| 1 | 1110 | 1120 | 1130 | 1140 | 1150 | 1160 |
| 2 | 1232 | 1254 | 1277 | 1300 | 1323 | 1346 |
| 3 | 1368 | 1405 | 1443 | 1482 | 1521 | 1561 |
| 4 | 1518 | 1574 | 1630 | 1689 | 1749 | 1811 |
| 5 | 1685 | 1762 | 1842 | 1925 | 2011 | 2100 |
| 6 | 1870 | 1974 | 2082 | 2195 | 2313 | 2436 |
| 7 | 2076 | 2211 | 2353 | 2502 | 2660 | 2826 |
| 8 | 2305 | 2476 | 2658 | 2853 | 3059 | 3278 |
| 9 | 2558 | 2773 | 3004 | 3252 | 3518 | 3803 |
| 10 | 2839 | 3106 | 3395 | 3707 | 4046 | 4411 |
| 11 | 3152 | 3479 | 3836 | 4226 | 4652 | 5117 |
| 12 | 3498 | 3896 | 4335 | 4818 | 5350 | 5936 |
| 13 | 3883 | 4363 | 4898 | 5492 | 6153 | 6886 |
| 14 | 4310 | 4887 | 5535 | 6261 | 7076 | 7988 |
| 15 | 4785 | 5474 | 6254 | 7138 | 8137 | 9266 |
| 16 | 5311 | 6130 | 7067 | 8137 | 9358 | 10748 |
| 17 | 5895 | 6866 | 7986 | 9276 | 10761 | 12468 |
| 18 | 6544 | 7690 | 9024 | 10575 | 12375 | 14463 |
| 19 | 7263 | 8613 | 10197 | 12056 | 14232 | 16777 |
| 20 | 8062 | 9646 | 11523 | 13743 | 16367 | 19461 |
| 21 | 8949 | 10804 | 13021 | 15668 | 18822 | 22574 |
| 22 | 9934 | 12100 | 14714 | 17861 | 21645 | 26186 |
| 23 | 11026 | 13552 | 16627 | 20362 | 24891 | 30376 |
| 24 | 12239 | 15179 | 18788 | 23212 | 28625 | 35236 |
| 25 | 13585 | 17000 | 21231 | 26462 | 32919 | 40874 |
| 26 | 15080 | 19040 | 23991 | 30167 | 37857 | 47414 |
| 27 | 16739 | 21325 | 27109 | 34390 | 43535 | 55000 |
| 28 | 18580 | 23884 | 30633 | 39204 | 50066 | 63800 |
| 29 | 20624 | 26750 | 34616 | 44693 | 57575 | 74009 |
| 30 | 22892 | 29960 | 39116 | 50950 | 66212 | 85850 |
| 31 | 25410 | 33555 | 44201 | 58083 | 76144 | 99586 |
| 32 | 28206 | 37582 | 49947 | 66215 | 87565 | 115520 |
| 33 | 31308 | 42092 | 56440 | 75485 | 100700 | 134003 |
| 34 | 34752 | 47143 | 63777 | 86053 | 115805 | 155443 |
| 35 | 38575 | 52800 | 72069 | 98100 | 133176 | 180314 |
| 36 | 42818 | 59136 | 81437 | 111834 | 153152 | 209164 |
| 37 | 47528 | 66232 | 92024 | 127491 | 176125 | 242631 |
| 38 | 52756 | 74180 | 103987 | 145340 | 202543 | 281452 |
| 39 | 58559 | 83081 | 117506 | 165687 | 232925 | 326484 |
| 40 | 65001 | 93051 | 132782 | 188884 | 267864 | 378721 |

## THE MAGIC OF COMPOUNDING INTEREST

If you had invested $1,000 per year at the beginning of each year and reinvested the earnings annually, here is the value which it will have increased to.

| Yr | 5% | 6% | 7% | 8% | 9% | 10% |
|---|---|---|---|---|---|---|
| 1 | 1050 | 1060 | 1070 | 1080 | 1090 | 1100 |
| 2 | 2153 | 2184 | 2215 | 2246 | 2278 | 2310 |
| 3 | 3310 | 3375 | 3440 | 3506 | 3573 | 3641 |
| 4 | 4526 | 4637 | 4751 | 4867 | 4985 | 5105 |
| 5 | 5802 | 5975 | 6153 | 6336 | 6523 | 6716 |
| 6 | 7142 | 7394 | 7654 | 7923 | 8200 | 8487 |
| 7 | 8549 | 8897 | 9260 | 9637 | 10028 | 10436 |
| 8 | 10027 | 10491 | 10978 | 11488 | 12021 | 12579 |
| 9 | 11578 | 12181 | 12816 | 13487 | 14193 | 14937 |
| 10 | 13207 | 13972 | 14784 | 15645 | 16560 | 17531 |
| 11 | 14917 | 15870 | 16888 | 17977 | 19141 | 20384 |
| 12 | 16713 | 17882 | 19141 | 20495 | 21953 | 23523 |
| 13 | 18599 | 20015 | 21550 | 23215 | 25019 | 26975 |
| 14 | 20579 | 22276 | 24129 | 26152 | 28361 | 30772 |
| 15 | 22657 | 24673 | 26888 | 29324 | 32003 | 34950 |
| 16 | 24840 | 27213 | 29840 | 32750 | 35974 | 39545 |
| 17 | 27132 | 29906 | 32999 | 36450 | 40301 | 44599 |
| 18 | 29539 | 32760 | 36379 | 40446 | 45018 | 50159 |
| 19 | 32066 | 35786 | 39995 | 44762 | 50160 | 56275 |
| 20 | 34719 | 38993 | 43865 | 49423 | 55765 | 63002 |
| 21 | 37505 | 42392 | 48006 | 54457 | 61873 | 70403 |
| 22 | 40430 | 45996 | 52436 | 59893 | 68532 | 78543 |
| 23 | 43502 | 49816 | 57177 | 65765 | 75790 | 87497 |
| 24 | 46727 | 53865 | 62249 | 72106 | 83701 | 97347 |
| 25 | 50113 | 58156 | 67676 | 78954 | 92324 | 108182 |
| 26 | 53669 | 62706 | 73484 | 86351 | 101723 | 120100 |
| 27 | 57403 | 67528 | 79698 | 94339 | 111968 | 133210 |
| 28 | 61323 | 72640 | 86347 | 102966 | 123135 | 147631 |
| 29 | 65439 | 78058 | 93461 | 112283 | 135308 | 163494 |
| 30 | 69761 | 83802 | 101073 | 122346 | 148575 | 180943 |
| 31 | 74299 | 89890 | 109218 | 133214 | 163037 | 200138 |
| 32 | 79064 | 96343 | 117933 | 144951 | 178800 | 221252 |
| 33 | 84067 | 103184 | 127259 | 157627 | 195982 | 244477 |
| 34 | 89320 | 110435 | 137237 | 171317 | 214711 | 270024 |
| 35 | 94836 | 118121 | 147913 | 186102 | 235125 | 298127 |
| 36 | 100628 | 126268 | 159337 | 202070 | 257376 | 329039 |
| 37 | 106710 | 134904 | 171561 | 219316 | 281630 | 363043 |
| 38 | 113095 | 144058 | 184640 | 237941 | 308066 | 400448 |
| 39 | 119800 | 153762 | 198635 | 258057 | 336882 | 441593 |
| 40 | 126840 | 164048 | 213610 | 279781 | 368292 | 486852 |

| Yr | 11% | 12% | 13% | 14% | 15% | 16% |
|---|---|---|---|---|---|---|
| 1 | 1110 | 1120 | 1130 | 1140 | 1150 | 1160 |
| 2 | 2342 | 2374 | 2407 | 2440 | 2473 | 2506 |
| 3 | 3710 | 3779 | 3850 | 3921 | 3993 | 4066 |
| 4 | 5228 | 5353 | 5480 | 5610 | 5742 | 5877 |
| 5 | 6913 | 7115 | 7323 | 7536 | 7754 | 7977 |
| 6 | 8783 | 9089 | 9405 | 9730 | 10067 | 10414 |
| 7 | 10859 | 11300 | 11757 | 12233 | 12727 | 13240 |
| 8 | 13164 | 13776 | 14416 | 15085 | 15786 | 16519 |
| 9 | 15722 | 16549 | 17420 | 18337 | 19304 | 20321 |
| 10 | 18561 | 19655 | 20814 | 22045 | 23349 | 24733 |
| 11 | 21713 | 23133 | 24650 | 26271 | 28002 | 29850 |
| 12 | 25212 | 27029 | 28985 | 31089 | 33352 | 35786 |
| 13 | 29095 | 31393 | 33883 | 36581 | 39505 | 42672 |
| 14 | 33405 | 36280 | 39417 | 42842 | 46580 | 50660 |
| 15 | 38190 | 41753 | 45672 | 49980 | 54717 | 59925 |
| 16 | 43501 | 47884 | 52739 | 58118 | 64075 | 70673 |
| 17 | 49396 | 54750 | 60725 | 67394 | 74836 | 83141 |
| 18 | 55939 | 62440 | 69749 | 77969 | 87212 | 97603 |
| 19 | 63203 | 71052 | 79947 | 90025 | 101444 | 114380 |
| 20 | 71265 | 80699 | 91470 | 103768 | 117810 | 133841 |
| 21 | 80214 | 91503 | 104491 | 119436 | 136632 | 156415 |
| 22 | 90148 | 103603 | 119205 | 137297 | 158276 | 182601 |
| 23 | 101174 | 117155 | 135831 | 157659 | 183168 | 212978 |
| 24 | 113413 | 132334 | 154620 | 180871 | 211793 | 248214 |
| 25 | 126999 | 149334 | 175850 | 207333 | 244712 | 289088 |
| 26 | 142079 | 168374 | 199841 | 237499 | 282569 | 336502 |
| 27 | 158817 | 189699 | 226950 | 271889 | 326104 | 391503 |
| 28 | 177397 | 213583 | 257583 | 311094 | 376170 | 455303 |
| 29 | 198021 | 240333 | 292199 | 355787 | 433745 | 529312 |
| 30 | 220913 | 270293 | 331315 | 406737 | 499957 | 615162 |
| 31 | 246324 | 303848 | 375516 | 464820 | 576100 | 714747 |
| 32 | 274529 | 341429 | 425463 | 531035 | 663666 | 830267 |
| 33 | 305837 | 383521 | 481903 | 606520 | 764365 | 964270 |
| 34 | 340590 | 430663 | 545681 | 692573 | 880170 | 1119713 |
| 35 | 379164 | 483463 | 617749 | 790673 | 1013346 | 1300027 |
| 36 | 421982 | 542599 | 699187 | 902507 | 1166498 | 1509191 |
| 37 | 469511 | 608831 | 791211 | 1029998 | 1342622 | 1751822 |
| 38 | 522267 | 683010 | 895198 | 1175338 | 1545165 | 2033273 |
| 39 | 580826 | 766091 | 1012704 | 1341025 | 1778090 | 2359757 |
| 40 | 645827 | 859142 | 1145486 | 1529909 | 2045954 | 2738478 |

# Inflation
# Table

## $10,000 INFLATED

This table shows the effect of various rates of inflation. It shows how much would be needed in any given year to equal the purchasing power of $10,000 under a given rate of inflation.

| Yrs | 4% | 5% | 6% | 7% | 8% | 9% | 10% | 11% | 12% |
|---|---|---|---|---|---|---|---|---|---|
| 1 | 10400 | 10500 | 10600 | 10700 | 10800 | 10900 | 11000 | 11100 | 11200 |
| 2 | 10816 | 11025 | 11236 | 11449 | 11664 | 11881 | 12100 | 12321 | 12544 |
| 3 | 11249 | 11576 | 11910 | 12250 | 12597 | 12950 | 13310 | 13676 | 14049 |
| 4 | 11699 | 12155 | 12625 | 13108 | 13605 | 14116 | 14641 | 15181 | 15735 |
| 5 | 12167 | 12763 | 13382 | 14026 | 14693 | 15386 | 16105 | 16851 | 17623 |
| 6 | 12653 | 13401 | 14185 | 15007 | 15869 | 16771 | 17716 | 18704 | 19738 |
| 7 | 13159 | 14071 | 15036 | 16058 | 17138 | 18280 | 19487 | 20762 | 22107 |
| 8 | 13686 | 14775 | 15938 | 17182 | 18509 | 19926 | 21436 | 23045 | 24760 |
| 9 | 14233 | 15513 | 16895 | 18385 | 19990 | 21719 | 23579 | 25580 | 27731 |
| 10 | 14802 | 16289 | 17908 | 19672 | 21589 | 23674 | 25937 | 28394 | 31058 |
| 11 | 15395 | 17103 | 18983 | 21049 | 23316 | 25804 | 28531 | 31518 | 34785 |
| 12 | 16010 | 17959 | 20122 | 22522 | 25182 | 28127 | 31384 | 34985 | 38960 |
| 13 | 16651 | 18856 | 21329 | 24098 | 27196 | 30658 | 34523 | 38833 | 43635 |
| 14 | 17317 | 19799 | 22609 | 25785 | 29372 | 33417 | 37975 | 43104 | 48871 |
| 15 | 18009 | 20789 | 23966 | 27590 | 31722 | 36425 | 41772 | 47846 | 54736 |
| 16 | 18730 | 21829 | 25404 | 29522 | 34259 | 39703 | 45950 | 53109 | 61304 |
| 17 | 19479 | 22920 | 26928 | 31588 | 37000 | 43276 | 50545 | 58951 | 68660 |
| 18 | 20258 | 24066 | 28543 | 33799 | 39960 | 47171 | 55599 | 65436 | 76900 |
| 19 | 21068 | 25270 | 30256 | 36165 | 43157 | 51417 | 61159 | 72633 | 86128 |
| 20 | 21911 | 26533 | 32071 | 38697 | 46610 | 56044 | 67275 | 80623 | 96463 |

# Investment Comparison Tables

## HOUSE / INVESTMENT COMPARISON

| DATE | INFLATION | | HOUSE PRICES | | TRUST CO. | | TEMPLETON GROWTH FUND | |
|---|---|---|---|---|---|---|---|---|
| | $ AMOUNT | RATE | AVERAGE PRICE*** | ANNUAL % CHAMGE | TRUST CO GIC | ANNUAL RATE** | CASHABLE VALUE | ANNUAL % CHANGE |
| Dec. 31/67 | $24,078.00 | | $24,078.00 | | $24,078.00 | | $22,211.96* | − 7.75% |
| Dec. 31/68 | 25,065.20 | 4.1% | 26,732.00 | + 11.02% | 25,712.90 | + 6.79% | 30,381.52 | + 36.78% |
| Dec. 31/69 | 26,218.20 | 4.6% | 28,929.00 | + 8.22% | 27,646.51 | + 7.52% | 36,381.86 | + 19.75% |
| Dec. 31/70 | 27,083.40 | 3.3% | 29,492.00 | + 1.95% | 30,026.87 | + 8.61% | 32,073.86 | − 11.94% |
| Dec. 31/71 | 27,868.82 | 2.9% | 30,426.00 | + 3.17% | 34,462.05 | + 8.11% | 38,628.05 | + 20.57% |
| Dec. 31/72 | 29,206.52 | 4.8% | 32,513.00 | + 6.86% | 34,747.38 | + 7.04% | 64,690.39 | + 67.47% |
| Dec. 31/73 | 31,397.01 | 7.5% | 40,605.00 | + 24.89% | 37,367.33 | + 7.54% | 58,292.51 | − 9.89% |
| Dec. 31/74 | 34,819.28 | 10.9% | 52,806.00 | + 30.05% | 40,592.13 | + 8.63% | 51,000.12 | − 12.51% |
| Dec. 31/75 | 38,579.76 | 10.8% | 57,581.00 | + 9.04% | 44,493.03 | + 9.61% | 71,940.77 | + 41.06% |
| Dec. 31/76 | 41,473.24 | 7.5% | 61,389.00 | + 6.61% | 48,942.33 | + 10.00% | 104,350.08 | + 45.05% |
| Dec. 31/77 | 45,413.20 | 9.5% | 64,559.00 | + 5.16% | 53,459.71 | + 9.23% | 136,646.42 | + 30.95% |
| Dec. 31/78 | 49,545.80 | 9.1% | 67,333.00 | + 4.30% | 58,137.44 | + 8.75% | 176,670.15 | + 29.29% |
| Dec. 31/79 | 54,401.29 | 9.8% | 70,830.00 | + 5.19% | 63,927.92 | + 9.96% | 220,290.01 | + 24.69% |
| Dec. 31/80 | 60,494.23 | 11.2% | 75,694.00 | + 6.87% | 71,049.49 | + 11.14% | 283,909.76 | + 28.88% |
| Dec. 31/81 | 68,056.01 | 12.5% | 90,203.00 | + 19.17% | 80,413.82 | + 13.18% | 281,354.58 | − 0.90% |
| Dec. 31/82 | 75,406.06 | 10.8% | 95,496.00 | + 5.87% | 93,392.61 | + 16.14% | 323,445.22 | + 14.96% |
| Dec. 31/83 | 79,779.61 | 5.8% | 101,626.00 | + 6.42% | 104,534.34 | + 11.93% | 435,098.50 | + 34.52% |
| Dec. 31/84 | 83,289.91 | 4.4% | 102,318.00 | + 0.68% | 115,591.30 | + 10.96% | 472,516.97 | + 8.60% |
| Dec. 31/85 | 86,621.51 | 4.0% | 109,094.00 | + 6.62% | 128,576.35 | + 10.85% | 628,275.92 | + 35.08% |
| Dec. 31/86 | 90,172.99 | 4.1% | 138,925.00 | + 27.34% | 141,601.13 | + 10.13% | 764,080.10 | + 19.71% |
| Dec. 31/87 | 94,140.60 | 4.4% | 189,105.00 | + 36.13% | 156,299.33 | + 10.13% | 725,112.02 | − 5.1% |
| Dec. 31/88 | 97,906.22 | 4.0% | 229,635.00 | + 21.43% | 172,320.01 | + 10.25% | 814,300.79 | + 12.3% |
| Dec. 31/89 | 102,801.53 | 5.0% | 273,698.00 | + 19.19% | 190,482.52 | + 10.54% | 986,118.25 | + 21.1% |
| Dec. 31/90 | 107,736.00 | 4.8% | 255,020.00 | − 6.82% | 210,254.60 | + 10.38% | 852,203.40 | − 13.58% |
| Dec. 31/91 | 113,769.21 | 5.6% | 234,313.00 | − 8.12% | 231,721.59 | + 10.21% | 1,110,676.70 | + 30.33% |
| Dec. 31/92 | 115,475.74 | 1.5% | 214,971.00 | − 8.25% | 250,259.31 | + 8.00% | 1,279,832.76 | + 15.23% |
| Dec. 31/93 | 117,544.30 | 1.8% | 206,490.00 | − 3.94% | 267,151.81 | + 6.75% | 1,744,412.03 | + 36.3% |
| Annual Compound Rate of Return (26 Years) | +6.35% | | + 8.62% | | + 9.70% | | + 17.90% | |

\* TEMPLETON GROWTH FUND – RESULTS AFTER 7.75% SALES CHARGE
\*\* GIC RATE – BANK OF CANADA REVIEW, AVERAGE 5 YEAR GIC RATE, JANUARY
\*\*\* AVERAGE PRICE OF HOUSES SOLD THROUGH TORONTO REAL ESTATE BOARD PHOTO MLS LISTINGS

## COMPARISON: $10,000 with (loaned to) Trust Company
### vs. $10,000 invested (owned) in Industrial Growth Fund or Templeton Growth Fund

| | TRUST COMPANY* | | INDUSTRIAL GROWTH FUND | | TEMPLETON GROWTH FUND | |
|---|---|---|---|---|---|---|
| | % INTEREST | YEAR-END VALUE | % ANNUAL CHANGE | YEAR-END** VALUE | % ANNUAL CHANGE | YEAR-END** VALUE |
| 1968 | 6.79% | $ 10,679 | + 35% | $ 12,285 | + 36% | $ 12,444 |
| 1969 | 7.52% | $ 11,482 | − 12% | $ 10,810 | + 20% | $ 14,932 |
| 1970 | 8.61% | $ 12,470 | − 2% | $ 10,594 | − 12% | $ 13,140 |
| 1971 | 8.11% | $ 13,482 | + 6% | $ 11,230 | + 21% | $ 15,900 |
| 1972 | 7.04% | $ 14,431 | + 42% | $ 15,946 | + 67% | $ 26,553 |
| 1973 | 7.54% | $ 15,519 | + 61% | $ 25,674 | − 10% | $ 23,898 |
| 1974 | 8.63% | $ 16,858 | + 1% | $ 25,931 | − 13% | $ 20,791 |
| 1975 | 9.61% | $ 18,478 | + 14% | $ 29,561 | + 41% | $ 29,316 |
| 1976 | 10.00% | $ 20,326 | + 16% | $ 34,291 | + 45% | $ 42,505 |
| 1977 | 9.23% | $ 22,202 | + 33% | $ 45,607 | + 31% | $ 55,685 |
| 1978 | 8.75% | $ 24,145 | + 16% | $ 52,905 | + 29% | $ 71,834 |
| 1979 | 9.96% | $ 26,550 | + 33% | $ 70,363 | + 25% | $ 89,793 |
| 1980 | 11.14% | $ 29,508 | + 23% | $ 86,547 | + 29% | $115,832 |
| 1981 | 13.18% | $ 33,397 | − 8% | $ 79,623 | − 1% | $114,673 |
| 1982 | 16.14% | $ 38,787 | + 32% | $105,102 | + 14.9% | $131,839 |
| 1983 | 11.93% | $ 43,414 | + 26.3% | $131,693 | + 34.5% | $177,323 |
| 1984 | 10.96% | $ 48,172 | + 5.6% | $139,068 | + 8.6% | $192,573 |
| 1985 | 10.85% | $ 53,399 | + 28.1% | $178,146 | + 35.1% | $260,166 |
| 1986 | 10.13% | $ 58,808 | + 7.6% | $191,685 | + 19.7% | $311,419 |
| 1987 | 10.38% | $ 64,912 | + 11.7% | $214,112 | − 5.1% | $295,536 |
| 1988 | 10.25% | $ 71,565 | + 17.5% | $251,582 | + 12.3% | $331,887 |
| 1989 | 10.54% | $ 79,108 | + 12.7% | $283,533 | + 21.1% | $401,915 |
| 1990 | 10.38% | $ 87,319 | − 15.0% | $241,002 | − 13.6% | $347,255 |
| 1991 | 10.21% | $ 96,234 | + 2.3% | $246,546 | + 30.3% | $452,473 |
| 1992 | 8.00% | $103,933 | − 4.8% | $237,711 | + 15.2% | $521,249 |
| 1993 | 6.25% | $110,948 | + 46.9% | $349,197 | + 36.3% | $710,462 |
| Equivalent Annual Compound Rate | 9.70% | | 14.64% | | 17.82% | |
| Value at end of 26 years | | $110,948 | | $349,197 | | $710,462 |

* Bank of Canada Review, Average 5 Year GIC Rate, January
** Results show deduction of standard commission

# Mutual
# Funds
# Performance
# Tables

**$10,000 INVESTED**

December 31, 1982 to December 31, 1993

| INVESTMENT FUND(S) | ANNUAL PERCENTAGE CHANGE IN VALUE | | | | | | | | | | | VALUE |
| --- | --- | --- | --- | --- | --- | --- | --- | --- | --- | --- | --- | --- |
| | 1983 | 1984 | 1985 | 1986 | 1987 | 1988 | 1989 | 1990 | 1991 | 1992 | 1993 | DEC. 31, 1993 |
| Templeton Growth | 34.5% | 8.6% | 35.1% | 19.7% | -5.1% | 12.3% | 21.1% | -13.6% | 30.3% | 15.2% | 36.3% | $53,888.76 |
| Bullock American | 25.1% | -10.4% | 34.2% | 29.1% | -2.3% | -4.0% | 41.9% | 10.5% | 81.9% | 4.3% | 20.3% | 65,183.43 |
| Cundill Value | 44.1% | 6.0% | 22.2% | 6.8% | 12.9% | 19.2% | 10.0% | -9.3% | 5.4% | 7.1% | 43.1% | 43,236.67 |
| AGF Special | 33.3% | -0.9% | 34.9% | 9.7% | -2.4% | 11.1% | 21.3% | -5.4% | 41.9% | 11.7% | 9.5% | 42,217.05 |
| AGF Japan | 33.3% | 11.8% | 45.1% | 54.7% | 27.0% | 1.1% | 12.4% | -20.5% | 3.1% | -11.8% | 20.6% | 42,091.32 |
| CI Pacific | 22.0% | 7.9% | 36.2% | 68.0% | 3.8% | 13.4% | 16.1% | -15.5% | 15.8% | 12.4% | 91.7% | 86,788.86 |
| Gold Fund | -5.1% | -20.9% | 16.1% | 34.0% | 22.6% | -29.7% | 10.1% | -2.7% | -11.3% | -5.9% | 115.4% | 19,385.84 |
| Industrial American | 23.2% | 4.7% | 31.7% | 12.5% | 1.1% | 9.5% | 16.9% | -11.0% | 16.9% | 14.6% | 23.4% | 36,389.81 |
| B/T International | 29.4% | 8.1% | 41.3% | 24.4% | -7.8% | 5.9% | 18.2% | -9.2% | 18.4% | 9.9% | 28.3% | 43,015.88 |
| United Amer. Equity | 24.4% | 15.5% | 34.9% | 16.4% | -5.2% | 9.4% | 26.6% | -6.6% | 23.1% | 16.1% | 4.0% | 41,124.17 |
| United Amer. Growth | 27.7% | 10.7% | 34.5% | 10.8% | -14.4% | 11.7% | 22.9% | -6.5% | 31.3% | 20.0% | 20.0% | 43,764.12 |
| Universal American | 19.0% | 2.2% | 39.2% | 10.7% | 4.1% | 7.9% | 18.8% | -9.1% | 13.8% | 17.3 | 32.1% | 40,084.85 |
| Trimark | 35.6% | 1.3% | 37.3% | 10.3% | -2.3% | 22.8% | 15.9% | -9.9% | 28.3% | 29.0% | 31.6% | 56,766.04 |

QUALIFY FOR TAX SAVINGS PROGRAMS: (RRSP's) (DPSP's) (RRIF's)

| | 1983 | 1984 | 1985 | 1986 | 1987 | 1988 | 1989 | 1990 | 1991 | 1992 | 1993 | DEC. 31, 1993 |
| --- | --- | --- | --- | --- | --- | --- | --- | --- | --- | --- | --- | --- |
| AGF Cdn Equity | 39.8% | 4.5% | 33.6% | 13.6% | -3.1% | 9.1% | 12.8% | -20.0% | 9.2% | 2.5% | 30.4% | $30,873.08 |
| Industrial Growth | 25.2% | 5.5% | 28.1% | 7.6% | 11.7% | 17.5% | 12.7% | -15.0% | 2.3% | -4.8% | 46.9% | 32,748.13 |
| B/S Canada Growth* | 35.0% | 5.8% | 37.3% | 25.4% | 10.4% | 12.0% | 13.6% | -0.7% | 13.6% | 7.3% | 34.0% | 56,025.41 |
| Jones Heward | 31.8% | 0.6% | 27.2% | 15.3% | -5.1% | 14.7% | 15.5% | -16.2% | 19.0% | 10.8% | 37.7% | 37,196.84 |
| B/T Cda. Cum. | 36.0% | -5.6% | 18.8% | 7.4% | -5.2% | 12.0% | 18.5% | -15.8% | 10.5% | 3.1% | 23.9% | 24,495.18 |
| Universal Equity | 27.5% | 2.7% | 30.9% | 7.7% | 17.1% | 16.8% | 8.9% | -18.4% | -1.9% | -4.1% | 56.5% | 33,033.59 |
| Dynamic Canada | 26.8% | -6.1% | 28.1% | 7.3% | 9.8% | 9.2% | 20.7% | -11.0% | 13.9% | 6.9% | 53.4% | 39,371.57 |
| United Cdn. Equity | 32.8% | 13.1% | 29.3% | 11.0% | -5.3% | 15.6% | 14.9% | -9.3% | 19.3% | 4.7% | 42.9% | 43,897.18 |
| United Cdn. Growth | 38.5& | 2.0% | 33.7% | 17.1% | -8.7% | 14.1% | 11.3% | -21.2% | 19.6% | 8.4% | 54.8% | 40,555.29 |
| Talvest Growth | 28.3% | 1.2% | 27.1% | 9.5% | 7.3% | 13.0% | 12.9% | -7.4% | 21.1% | -1.3% | 19.7% | 32,772.18 |
| Trimark Canadian | 42.9% | 4.0% | 30.2% | 5.3% | 6.6% | 19.1% | 18.8% | -12.1% | 20.2% | 6.6% | 37.9% | 47,731.51 |
| 10% Investment | 10.0% | 10.0% | 10.0% | 10.0% | 10.0% | 10.0% | 10.0% | 10.0% | 10.0% | 10.0% | 10.0% | 28,531.17 |

## 15 YEAR MONTHLY SAVINGS PLAN

Examples of Various Amounts Invested Monthly in
TEMPLETON GROWTH FUND LTD.

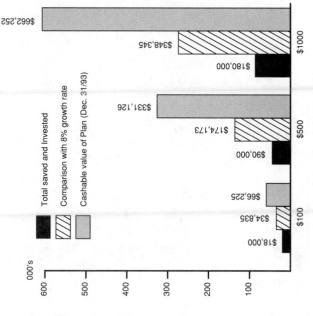

| Amount Invested Each Month | Total Amount Saved and Invested | Cashable Value of Plan at Dec. 31, 1993 | Comparison If Growth was at 8% Rate |
|---|---|---|---|
| 50 | $ 9,000 | $ 33,133 | $ 17,417 |
| 60 | 10,800 | 39,735 | 20,901 |
| 70 | 12,600 | 46,357 | 24,384 |
| 80 | 14,400 | 52,981 | 27,868 |
| 100 | 18,000 | 66,225 | 34,835 |
| 120 | 21,600 | 79,470 | 41,801 |
| 150 | 27,000 | 99,338 | 52,252 |
| 200 | 36,000 | 132,450 | 69,669 |
| 250 | 45,000 | 165,563 | 87,086 |
| 300 | 54,000 | 199,676 | 104,504 |
| 400 | 72,000 | 264,901 | 139,338 |
| 500 | 90,000 | 331,126 | 174,173 |
| 750 | 135,000 | 496,690 | 261,259 |
| 1000 | 180,000 | 662,252 | 348,345 |

Period: January 1, 1979 through December 31, 1993 = 15 Years
All dividends reinvested.
Average annual compound rates of return for Templeton Growth Fund
Ltd. to December 31, 1 year 36.3%; 3 years 27.0%; 5 years 16.5%; 10
years 14.9%; 15 years 16.5%; 20 years 18%

**$100,000** INVESTED JAN. 2, 1968 TAKING $9,000 ANNUAL INCOME — INCREASED YEARLY BY INFLATION RATE

| | INDUSTRIAL GROWTH FUND | 26-YEAR RESULTS COMPARED | | 10% INVESTMENT |
| --- | --- | --- | --- | --- |
| | Cash Value Remaining | Canadian Consumer Price Index % Change | 9% per Year* Indexed Withdrawl | Cash Value Remaining |
| 1968 | $120,600 | 4.0% | $ 9,000 | $ 101,000 |
| 1969 | 97,009 | 4.6% | 9,360. | 101,740 |
| 1970 | 84,987 | 3.3% | 9,791 | 102,124 |
| 1971 | 79,716 | 2.9% | 10,114 | 102,223 |
| 1972 | 103,061 | 4.8% | 10,407 | 102,040 |
| 1973 | 155,228 | 7.5% | 10,906 | 101,339 |
| 1974 | 144,606 | 10.9% | 11,724 | 99,750 |
| 1975 | 155,181 | 10.8% | 13,002 | 96,724 |
| 1976 | 162,047 | 7.5% | 14,407 | 91,991 |
| 1977 | 199,387 | 9.5% | 15,487 | 85,705 |
| 1978 | 215,328 | 9.5% | 16,958 | 77,320 |
| 1979 | 267,601 | 9.8% | 18,570 | 66,485 |
| 1980 | 306,084 | 11.2% | 20,389 | 52,748 |
| 1981 | 259,536 | 12.5% | 22,673 | 35,354 |
| 1982 | 320,714 | 10.8% | 25,507 | 13,388 |
| 1983 | 373,272 | 5.8% | 28,262 | - 13,528 |
| 1984 | 363,901 | 4.4% | 29,901 | - 43,442 |
| 1985 | 434,941 | 4.0% | 31,217 | - 74,631 |
| 1986 | 434,531 | 4.2% | 32,465 | - 107,088 |
| 1987 | 452,659 | 4.4% | 33,829 | - 140,908 |
| 1988 | 496,558 | 4.0% | 35,317 | - 176,216 |
| 1989 | 522,890 | 5.0% | 36,730 | - 212,936 |
| 1990 | 405,890 | 4.8% | 38,567 | - 251,492 |
| 1991 | 374,808 | 5.6% | 40,418 | - 291,899 |
| 1992 | 314,136 | 1.5% | 42,681 | - 334,580 |
| 1993 | 418,144 (93) | 1.8% | 43,321 (93) | - 377,901 (93) |
| TOTALS | $418,144 | 6.35% AV | $611,004 | RAN OUT OF MONEY |

* Systematic withdrawl plan beginning with 9% first year (indexed to inflation thereafter).

NOTE: Purchasing power of Canadian dollar during this period declined from $1.00 to 20.47¢
(i.e. $4.89 today required to make a purchase similar to $1.00 in 1967)

**$100,000** INVESTED JAN. 2, 1964 TAKING $9,000 ANNUAL INCOME – INCREASED YEARLY BY INFLATION RATE

| | TEMPLETON GROWTH FUND | 30-YEAR RESULTS COMPARED | | 10% INVESTMENT |
|---|---|---|---|---|
| | Cash Value Remaining | Canaadian Consumer Price Index % Change | 9% per Year* Indexed Withdrawl | Cash Value Remaining |
| 1964 | $ 114,264 | 1.8% | $ 9,000 | $ 101,000 |
| 1965 | 130,240 | 2.4% | 9162 | 101,938 |
| 1966 | 114,086 | 3.7% | 9382 | 102,750 |
| 1967 | 119,541 | 3.6% | 9729 | 103,297 |
| 1968 | 153,107 | 4.0% | 10,079 | 103,548 |
| 1969 | 173,108 | 4.6% | 10,482 | 103,420 |
| 1970 | 141,665 | 3.3% | 10,965 | 102,798 |
| 1971 | 159,719 | 2.9% | 11,326 | 101,752 |
| 1972 | 255,875 | 4.8% | 11,655 | 100,273 |
| 1973 | 218,355 | 7.5% | 12,214 | 98,087 |
| 1974 | 177,712 | 10.9% | 13,130 | 94,765 |
| 1975 | 236,420 | 10.8% | 14,562 | 89,681 |
| 1976 | 326,794 | 7.5% | 16,134 | 82,516 |
| 1977 | 410,428 | 9.5% | 17,344 | 73,424 |
| 1978 | 510,871 | 9.5% | 18,992 | 61,776 |
| 1979 | 615,238 | 9.8% | 20,796 | 47,159 |
| 1980 | 768,362 | 11.2% | 22,834 | 29,042 |
| 1981 | 736,055 | 12.5% | 25,392 | 6,557 |
| 1982 | 817,897 | 10.8% | 28,566 | – 21,349 |
| 1983 | 1,068,420 | 5.8% | 31,651 | – 52,955 |
| 1984 | 1,126,818 | 4.4% | 33,487 | – 86,436 |
| 1985 | 1,487,371 | 4.0% | 34,960 | – 121,391 |
| 1986 | 1,744,024 | 4.2% | 36,359 | – 157,744 |
| 1987 | 1,617,194 | 4.4% | 37,886 | – 195,623 |
| 1988 | 1,776,556 | 4.0% | 39,553 | – 235,169 |
| 1989 | 2,112,051 | 5.0% | 41,135 | – 276,297 |
| 1990 | 1,782,043 | 4.8% | 43,191 | – 319,481 |
| 1991 | 2,276,738 | 5.6% | 45,265 | – 364,738 |
| 1992 | 2,575,686 | 1.5% | 47,799 | – 412,537 |
| 1993 | 3,462,143 | 1.8% | 48,516 | – 461,053 |
| TOTALS | $3,462,143 | 5.89% AV | $721,546 | RAN OUT OF MONEY |

* Systematic withdrawal plan beginning with 9% first year (indexed to inflation thereafter).

**LONG TERM INVESTMENT RESULTS**
TEMPLETON GROWTH FUND, LTD.

| Date of Investment Jan. 1st | End of Period Dec. 31st | Cost of Investment* | Total Value End of Period | Compounded Annual Average |
|---|---|---|---|---|
| **10 YEAR PERIODS** | | | | |
| 1964 | 1973 | $ 10,000 | $ 44,724 | 16.2% |
| 1965 | 1974 | 10,000 | 30,586 | 11.8% |
| 1966 | 1975 | 10,000 | 35,312 | 13.4% |
| 1967 | 1976 | 10,000 | 53,225 | 18.2% |
| 1968 | 1977 | 10,000 | 61,657 | 19.9% |
| 1969 | 1978 | 10,000 | 58,276 | 19.3% |
| 1970 | 1979 | 10,000 | 60,660 | 19.8% |
| 1971 | 1980 | 10,000 | 88,752 | 24.4% |
| 1972 | 1981 | 10,000 | 72,809 | 22.0% |
| 1973 | 1982 | 10,000 | 49,945 | 17.4% |
| 1974 | 1983 | 10,000 | 68,463 | 21.2% |
| 1975 | 1984 | 10,000 | 92,642 | 24.9% |
| 1976 | 1985 | 10,000 | 88,639 | 24.4% |
| 1977 | 1986 | 10,000 | 73,173 | 22.0% |
| 1978 | 1987 | 10,000 | 52,993 | 18.1% |
| 1979 | 1988 | 10,000 | 46,108 | 16.5% |
| 1980 | 1989 | 10,000 | 44,777 | 16.2% |
| 1981 | 1990 | 10,000 | 30,013 | 11.6% |
| 1982 | 1991 | 10,000 | 39,463 | 14.7% |
| 1983 | 1992 | 10,000 | 39,566 | 14.7% |
| 1984 | 1993 | 10,000 | 40,119 | 14.9% |
| **15 YEAR PERIODS** | | | | |
| 1964 | 1978 | 10,000 | 135,453 | 19.0% |
| 1965 | 1979 | 10,000 | 132,167 | 18.8% |
| 1966 | 1980 | 10,000 | 139,300 | 19.2% |
| 1967 | 1981 | 10,000 | 143,499 | 19.4% |
| 1968 | 1982 | 10,000 | 145,912 | 19.6% |
| 1969 | 1983 | 10,000 | 143,459 | 19.4% |
| 1970 | 1984 | 10,000 | 130,047 | 18.7% |
| 1971 | 1985 | 10,000 | 183,125 | 21.4% |
| 1972 | 1986 | 10,000 | 197,609 | 22.0% |
| 1993 | 1987 | 10,000 | 111,841 | 17.5% |
| 1974 | 1988 | 10,000 | 139,646 | 19.2% |
| 1975 | 1989 | 10,000 | 193,491 | 21.8% |
| 1976 | 1990 | 10,000 | 118,397 | 17.9% |
| 1977 | 1991 | 10,000 | 106,394 | 17.1% |
| 1978 | 1992 | 10,000 | 93,633 | 16.1% |
| 1979 | 1993 | 10,000 | 98,458 | 16.47% |

Continued next page

LONG TERM INVESTMENT RESULTS CONTINUED
TEMPLETON GROWTH FUND, LTD.

| Date of Investment Jan. 1st | End of Period Dec. 31st | Cost of Investment* | Total Value End of Period | Compounded Annual Average |
|---|---|---|---|---|
| | | **20 YEAR PERIODS** | | |
| 1964 | 1983 | $ 10,000 | $ 333,445 | 19.2% |
| 1965 | 1984 | 10,000 | 283,350 | 18.2% |
| 1966 | 1985 | 10,000 | 313,005 | 18.8% |
| 1967 | 1986 | 10,000 | 289,467 | 20.1% |
| 1968 | 1987 | 10,000 | 325,739 | 19.0% |
| 1969 | 1988 | 10,000 | 268,700 | 17.9% |
| 1970 | 1989 | 10,000 | 271,615 | 17.9% |
| 1971 | 1990 | 10,000 | 244,602 | 17.3% |
| 1972 | 1991 | 10,000 | 287,322 | 18.3% |
| 1973 | 1992 | 10,000 | 197,609 | 16.1% |
| 1974 | 1993 | 10,000 | 297,902 | 18.4% |

* Assumed $10,000 Investments with dividends and capital gains distributions re-invested for various 10, 15 and 20 year periods.

## EXAMPLE OF A $100 MONTHLY SAVINGS PLAN

$100 PER MONTH (LESS 8.75% SALES FEE) INVESTED IN **CUNDILL VALUE FUND LTD.** BEGINNING DEC. 31, 1974

| Date | Cumulative Deposit | Total Number Shares Held | Cashable Value | Comparative Investment Earning 10% |
|---|---|---|---|---|
| Dec. 31, 1974 | $ 100 | 45 | $ 91 | $ 100 |
| Dec. 31, 1975 | 1,300 | 501 | 1,338 | 1,378 |
| Dec. 31, 1976 | 2,500 | 863 | 3,029 | 2,789 |
| Dec. 31, 1977 | 3,700 | 1,157 | 4,918 | 4,348 |
| Dec. 31, 1978 | 4,900 | 1,362 | 8,197 | 6,070 |
| Dec. 31, 1979 | 6,100 | 1,514 | 11,851 | 7,973 |
| Dec. 31, 1980 | 7,300 | 1,876 | 14,931 | 10,075 |
| Dec. 31, 1981 | 8,500 | 2,494 | 18,883 | 12,397 |
| Dec. 31, 1982 | 9,700 | 2,795 | 25,019 | 14,962 |
| Dec. 31, 1983 | 10,900 | 3,218 | 37,267 | 17,795 |
| Dec. 31, 1984 | 12,100 | 3,720 | 40,618 | 20,926 |
| Dec. 31, 1985 | 13,300 | 4,035 | 50,963 | 24,384 |
| Dec. 31, 1986 | 14,500 | 4,319 | 55,544 | 28,205 |
| Dec. 31, 1987 | 15,700 | 4,905 | 63,817 | 32,425 |
| Dec. 31, 1988 | 16,900 | 5,920 | 77,139 | 37,087 |
| Dec. 31, 1989 | 18,100 | 6,502 | 85,959 | 42,238 |
| Dec. 31, 1990 | 19,300 | 7,399 | 78,948 | 47,928 |
| Dec. 31, 1991 | 20,500 | 8,077 | 84,324 | 54,213 |
| Dec. 31, 1992 | 21,700 | 8,301 | 91,356 | 61,157 |
| Dec. 31, 1993 | $ 22,900 | 8,443 | $ 132,305 | $ 68,828 |

Summary of Investment

Total Invested at Dec. 31, 1974    $ 22,900
Cashable Value at March 31, 1993    132,305

Total Gain Since Dec. 31, 1974    109,405

## EXAMPLE OF A $10,000 CASH INVESTMENT

INVESTED (LESS 8.75% SALES FEE) INVESTED IN **CUNDILL VALUE FUND LTD.** ON DEC. 31, 1974

| Date | Years Capital Invested | Cashable Value | $10,000 Investment Earning 10% | Growth Needed to Match Inflation |
|------|------------------------|----------------|--------------------------------|----------------------------------|
| Dec. 31, 1974 | $10,000 | $9,125 | $10,000 | $10,000 |
| Dec. 31, 1975 | 1 | 12,061 | 11,000 | 10,952 |
| Dec. 31, 1976 | 2 | 15,856 | 12,100 | 11,595 |
| Dec. 31, 1977 | 3 | 19,199 | 13,310 | 12,690 |
| Dec. 31, 1978 | 4 | 27,191 | 14,641 | 13,762 |
| Dec. 31, 1979 | 5 | 35,371 | 16,105 | 15,095 |
| Dec. 31, 1980 | 6 | 40,988 | 17,716 | 16,786 |
| Dec. 31, 1981 | 7 | 48,696 | 19,487 | 18,833 |
| Dec. 31, 1982 | 8 | 61,181 | 21,436 | 20,571 |
| Dec. 31, 1983 | 9 | 88,185 | 23,579 | 21,500 |
| Dec. 31, 1984 | 10 | 93,435 | 25,937 | 22,310 |
| Dec. 31, 1985 | 11 | 114,123 | 28,531 | 23,286 |
| Dec. 31, 1986 | 12 | 122,204 | 31,384 | 24,262 |
| Dec. 31, 1987 | 13 | 137,993 | 34,523 | 25,262 |
| Dec. 31, 1988 | 14 | 164,283 | 37,975 | 26,262 |
| Dec. 31, 1989 | 15 | 180,942 | 41,772 | 27,619 |
| Dec. 31, 1990 | 16 | 163,770 | 45,950 | 29,000 |
| Dec. 31, 1991 | 17 | 172,613 | 50,545 | 30,095 |
| Dec. 31, 1992 | 18 | 185,111 | 55,599 | 30,738 |
| Dec. 31, 1993 | 19 | 264,947 | 61,159 | 31,291 |

Summary of Investment

| | |
|---|---|
| Total Invested at Dec. 31, 1974 | $ 10,000 |
| Cashable Value at March 31, 1993 | 264,947 |
| Total Gain Since Dec. 31, 1974 | 254,947 |

## EXAMPLE OF A $10,000- CASH INVESTMENT
INVESTED ON JAN. 1, 1964 WITH ALL DIVIDENDS REINVESTED TEMPLETON GROWTH FUND, LTD.

| DATE | DIVIDENDS REINVESTED EACH YEAR | TEMPLETON'S SHARE VALUE | CASHABLE VALUE | % CHANGE REPORTED IN FINANCIAL POST | COMPARATIVE GROWTH AT 12% |
|---|---|---|---|---|---|
| Jan. 01/64 | | $10.61 | $ 9,150.00 | | $10,000 |
| Dec. 31/64 | $ 120.74 | 13.39 | 11,692.44 | +27.8% | 11,200 |
| Dec. 31/65 | 179.71 | 16.15 | 14,301.20 | +22.3% | 12,544 |
| Dec. 31/66 | 239.71 | 15.28 | 13,752.38 | - 3.8% | 14,049 |
| Dec. 31/67 | 242.74 | 16.98 | 16,534.68 | + 13% | 15,735 |
| Dec. 31/68 | 246.10 | 22.92 | 21,249.43 | + 36.8 | 17,623 |
| Dec. 31/69 | 352.67 | 27.03 | 25,460.23 | +19.8% | 19,738 |
| Dec. 30/70 | 370.93 | 23.43 | 22,430.66 | -11.9% | 22,107 |
| Dec. 30/71 | 801.49 | 26.97 | 26,665.70 | | |
| Oct. 25/71 | Valuation Day | 5.48* | Shares Split 5 for 1 * | | |
| Dec. 31/71 | | | 27,090.85 | +20.8% | 24,760 |
| Dec. 31/72 | 1,063.86 | 8.91 | 46,376.79 | +67.5% | 27,731 |
| Dec. 31/73 | 4,348.23 | 7.30 | 40,894.26 | - 9.9% | 31,058 |
| Dec. 31/74 | 1,440.26 | 6.17 | 35,758.46 | -12.6% | 34,785 |
| Dec. 31/75 | 1,024.66 | 8.53 | 50,506.82 | +41.2% | 38,960 |
| Dec. 31/76 | 1,329.50 | 12.09 | 73,260.21 | +45.0% | 43,635 |
| Dec. 31/77 | 5,532.39 | 14.73 | 95,931.69 | +30.9% | 48,871 |
| Dec. 31/78 | 1,380.69 | 18.81 | 124,027.50 | +29.3% | 54,736 |
| Mar. 2/79 | | 7.59** | Shares Split 3 for 1 ** | | |
| Dec. 31/79 | 3,896.88 | 9.06 | 154,647.29 | +24.7% | 61,304 |
| Dec. 31/80 | 11,809.43 | 8.81 | 199,315.86 | +28.9% | 68,660 |
| Dec. 31/81 | 3,970.92 | 8.81 | 197,514.05 | - 0.9% | 76,900 |
| Dec. 31/82 | 15,341.53 | 9.28 | 226,858.17 | +14.9% | 86,128 |
| Dec. 31/83 | 5,414.77 | 12.24 | 305,150.97 | +34.5% | 96,463 |
| Dec. 31/84 | 15,498.87 | 12.60 | 331,382.70 | + 8.6% | 106,038 |
| Dec. 31/85 | 26,013.51 | 15.88 | 447,756.42 | +35.1% | 121,003 |
| Dec. 31/86 | 34,621.44 | 17.77 | 536,164.67 | +19.7% | 135,523 |
| Dec. 31/87 | 14,875.72 | 16.41 | 508,055.31 | - 5.2% | 151,786 |
| Dec. 31/88 | 16,718.45 | 17.89 | 571,721.91 | +12.5% | 170,000 |
| Jun. 31/89 | 13,741.76 | 19.62 | 640,750.37 | | |
| Oct. 30/89 | | 5.30*** | Shares Split 4 for 1 *** | | |
| Dec. 29/89 | 18,288.48 | | 692,350.04 | +21.1% | 190,401 |
| Dec. 31/90 | 28,171.29 | 4.46 | 598,304.98 | -13.6% | 213,249 |
| Dec. 31/91 | 61,489.84 | 5.58 | 779,803.62 | +30.3% | 238,838 |
| Dec. 31/92 | 42,073.04 | 5.98 | 898,559.80 | +15.2% | 267,499 |
| Dec. 31/93 | | 7.81 | 1,224,799.30 | +36.3% | 299,599 |
| TOTALS | $330,599.61 | $7.81 | 17.38% AV. | +17.4% AV. | 12% AV. |

Cash Value at December 31, 1993    1,244,799
Amount Invested    10,000
Gain in 30 Years    1,214,799

* 5 for 1 Share Split Oct. 25, 1971
** 3 for 1 Share Split Mar. 2, 1979
*** 4 for 1 Share Split Oct. 30/89

# The dollar cost averaging program

$1,200 invested annually under 3 different stock market conditions over a 10 year period

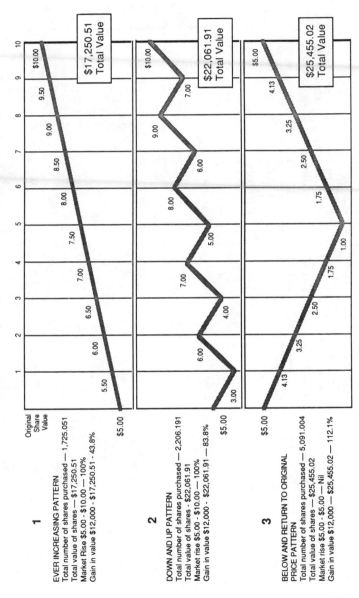

Original
Share
Value

**1**

EVER INCREASING PATTERN
Total number of shares purchased — 1,725.051
Total value of shares — $17,250.51
Market Rise $5.00 - $10.00 — 100%
Gain in value $12,000 - $17,250.51 - 43.8%

**$17,250.51
Total Value**

**2**

DOWN AND UP PATTERN
Total number of shares purchased — 2,206.191
Total value of shares - $22,061.91
Market rise $5.00 - $10.00. — 100%
Gain in value $12,000 - $22,061.91 - 83.8%

**$22,061.91
Total Value**

**3**

BELOW AND RETURN TO ORIGINAL
PRICE PATTERN
Total number of shares purchased — 5,091.004
Total value of shares — $25,455.02
Market rise $5.00 - $5.00 — Nil
Gain in value $12,000 — $25,455.02 — 112.1%

**$25,455.02
Total Value**

# Registered Retirement Savings Plan — Mr. A.

Industrial Growth Fund **Annual** Contributions.
Maximum Deductible Invested on December 31 each year.

| DATE | MAXIMUM ANNUAL DEPOSITS | INDUSTRIAL GROWTH FUND | 5-YEAR G.I.C. | NON-CHEQUABLE SAVINGS DEPOSIT | TO MATCH IMFLATION YOU NEED |
|---|---|---|---|---|---|
| Ded. 67 | $ 2,500 | $ 2,500 | $ 2,500 | $ 2,500 | $ 2,500 |
| Dec. 68 | 2,500 | 5,897 | 5,174 | 5,126 | 5,102 |
| Dec. 69 | 2,500 | 7,641 | 8,082 | 7,941 | 7,836 |
| Dec. 70 | 2,500 | 9,969 | 11,273 | 10,944 | 10,450 |
| Dec. 71 | 2,500 | 13,101 | 14,650 | 13,947 | 13,477 |
| Dec. 72 | 4,000 | 22,568 | 19,763 | 18,516 | 18,162 |
| Dec. 73 | 4,000 | 40,397 | 25,376 | 23,548 | 23,819 |
| Dec. 74 | 4,000 | 44,541 | 31,820 | 29,629 | 30,787 |
| Dec. 75 | 4,000 | 54,930 | 38,859 | 35,771 | 37,707 |
| Dec. 76 | 5,500 | 69,310 | 48,286 | 44,176 | 45,402 |
| Dec. 77 | 5,500 | 97,452 | 58,122 | 52,400 | 55,213 |
| Dec. 78 | 5,500 | 119,564 | 68,973 | 61,711 | 65,369 |
| Dec. 79 | 5,500 | 164,849 | 81,581 | 73,758 | 77,251 |
| Dec. 80 | 5,500 | 207,881 | 97,026 | 87,979 | 91,407 |
| Dec. 81 | 5,500 | 196,550 | 117,298 | 108,020 | 107,936 |
| Dec. 82 | 5,500 | 266,602 | 139,985 | 126,093 | 123,490 |
| Dec. 83 | 5,500 | 339,210 | 161,723 | 140,428 | 134,547 |
| Dec. 84 | 5,500 | 363,425 | 186,494 | 157,080 | 145,128 |
| Dec. 85 | 5,500 | 471,147 | 212,262 | 172,407 | 156,951 |
| Dec. 86 | 7,500 | 514,303 | 240,437 | 190,312 | 170,996 |
| Dec. 87 | 7,500 | 581,750 | 270,807 | 207,176 | 185,595 |
| Dec. 88 | 7,500 | 690,941 | 305,576 | 227,089 | 200,471 |
| Dec. 89 | 7500 | 786,537 | 344,605 | 253,641 | 218,195 |
| Dec. 90 | 7,500 | 676,342 | 390,608 | 284,303 | 236,168 |
| Dec. 91 | 11,500 | 703,148 | 438,967 | 308,801 | 256,643 |
| Dec. 92 | 12,500 | 681,827 | 485,844 | 328,386 | 274,532 |
| Dec. 93 | 12,500 | **1,013,926** | **530,538** | **343,426** | **292,248** |

| Total Deposited | $157,500 |
|---|---|

(All applicable acquisition and trustee fees deducted from Industrial Growth Fund. All dividends and interest income reinvested).
Sources: Interest rates — Bank of Canada; inflation — Stats Can Consumer Price Index

# Registered Retirement Savings Plan — Mr. B.

Industrial Growth Fund **Monthly** Contributions.
Maximum Deductible Invested on December 31 each year.

| DATE | MAXIMUM MONTHLY DEPOSITS | TOTAL ANNUAL DEPOSITS | INDUSTRIAL GROWTH FUND | 5-YEAR G.I.C. | NON-CHEQUABLE SAVINGS DEPOSIT | TO MATCH IMFLATION YOU NEED |
|---|---|---|---|---|---|---|
| Dec. 67 | $ 2,500 | $ 2,500 | $ 2,500 | $ 2,500 | $ 2,500 | $ 2,500 |
| Dec. 68 | 208 | 2,500 | 6,374 | 5,254 | 5,184 | 5,149 |
| Dec. 69 | 208 | 2,500 | 7,777 | 8,260 | 8,076 | 7,934 |
| Dec. 70 | 208 | 2,500 | 10,177 | 11,562 | 11,157 | 10,552 |
| Dec. 71 | 208 | 2,500 | 13,278 | 15,050 | 14,220 | 13,638 |
| Dec. 72 | 333 | 4,000 | 23,060 | 20,334 | 18,874 | 18,434 |
| Dec. 73 | 333 | 4,000 | 42,038 | 26,146 | 24,040 | 24,276 |
| Dec. 74 | 333 | 4,000 | 45,978 | 32,846 | 30,333 | 31,523 |
| Dec. 75 | 333 | 4,000 | 56,402 | 40,159 | 36,655 | 38,684 |
| Dec. 76 | 458 | 5,500 | 71,428 | 49,968 | 45,335 | 46,577 |
| Dec. 77 | 458 | 5,500 | 101,151 | 60,177 | 53,781 | 56,722 |
| Dec. 78 | 458 | 5,500 | 124,310 | 71,450 | 63,390 | 67,202 |
| Dec. 79 | 458 | 5,500 | 171,987 | 84,576 | 75,889 | 79,492 |
| Dec. 80 | 458 | 5,500 | 217,143 | 100,692 | 90,652 | 94,184 |
| Dec. 81 | 458 | 5,500 | 204,902 | 121,915 | 111,541 | 111,312 |
| Dec. 82 | 458 | 5,500 | 279,447 | 145,617 | 130,279 | 127,365 |
| Dec. 83 | 458 | 5,500 | 355,705 | 168,291 | 145,081 | 138,708 |
| Dec. 84 | 458 | 5,500 | 381,145 | 194,143 | 162,300 | 149,523 |
| Dec. 85 | 458 | 5,500 | 494,436 | 221,106 | 178,103 | 161,640 |
| Ded. 86 | 625 | 7500 | 539,589 | 250,362 | 196,537 | 176,020 |
| Dec. 87 | 625 | 7500 | 609,519 | 282,007 | 213,877 | 190,951 |
| Dec. 88 | 625 | 7,500 | 723,960 | 318,247 | 234,411 | 206,159 |
| Dec. 89 | 625 | 7,500 | 823,967 | 358,928 | 261,867 | 224,304 |
| Dec. 90 | 625 | 7,500 | 707,733 | 406,910 | 293,583 | 242,703 |
| Dec. 91 | 958 | 11,500 | 734,861 | 457,288 | 318,709 | 263,426 |
| Dec. 92 | 1,042 | 12,500 | 711,706 | 506,028 | 338,645 | 281,531 |
| Dec. 93 | 1,042 | 12,500 | **1,059,624** | **552,420** | **353,800** | **299,458** |

Total Deposited     $157,500

(All applicable acquisition and trustee fees deducted from Industrial Growth Fund. All dividends and interest income reinvested).
Sources: Interest rates — Bank of Canada; inflation — Stats Can Consumer Price Index